Nelson

OVERLEAF LEFT
Horatio Nelson in 1801, the year of
Copenhagen; portrait by John Hoppner.
OVERLEAF RIGHT
Embroidered portrait of Emma Hamilton
and Nelson with Merton Place in
the background, said to be by Emma.
END PAPERS
The battle of Cape St Vincent,
1797, by J.Luny.

Nelson

Roy Hattersley

Saturday Review Press
New York

Designed by Sheila Sherwen *for*
George Weidenfeld and
Nicolson Limited,
11 St John's Hill,
London SW11 *and*
Saturday Review Press,
201 Park Avenue South,
New York, N.Y.10003

Filmset by Cox & Wyman Ltd
London, Fakenham and Reading

ISBN 0–8415–0288–9

Library of Congress
Catalog Card No. 73–87558

Printed in Great Britain

Contents

THE TIMES
For 7th NOVEMBER. 1805
BATTLE OF
TRAFALGAR
CAPTURE OF
FRENCH AND
SPANISH FLEETS
DEATH OF NELSON
List of Killed and Wounded

To My Father

Introduction

FROM TIME TO TIME the sombre landscape of history is illuminated briefly as a man of destiny flashes like a comet across the scene. Horatio Nelson was such a man. He loved his country; he worshipped God (and, like many distinguished martial figures before and since, believed Him to be a personal ally); he was convinced from an early age that he had been singled out for glory. He carved for himself a unique and pre-eminent place in naval history. He was a post-captain at the age of twenty-one, and an admiral at the age of thirty-nine. His personal courage became a legend in his own time; the planning and execution of his battles was bold and imaginative. His greatest battle, Trafalgar, shares with Waterloo the summit of achievement in British arms; and he himself shares with Wellington a sacred corner in the pantheon of national heroes.

One of the most interesting patterns to emerge from a study of military history is the frequency with which great war leaders turn out to be notably unattractive men. It is often difficult to explain how people with such glaring defects of character and personality could have risen to the top of a profession in which human relationships play such a vital part. Roy Hattersley's absorbing account of the life of England's greatest sailor provides an interesting example of this paradox.

Much about Nelson was uncouth and even vulgar. His vanity was consuming; his egotism often abrasive. His reputation as a difficult colleague kept him ashore for six years of his career, during which England and France were at peace and, as Roy Hattersley writes, 'awkward officers were not in great demand'. Yet, like Napoleon, he was capable of inspiring among his men a loyalty and devotion which few military leaders in history have been able to command; and when he died in action the effect was shattering. His death, as Robert Southey wrote in his *Life of Nelson* 'was felt in England as something more than a public calamity; men started at the

7

Introduction

intelligence, and turned pale, as if they had heard of the loss of a dear friend'. He was not only a brilliant naval tactician, he was a great leader of men; and, like Field Marshal Montgomery a century and a half later, he insisted before embarking upon any action that everyone under his command should be fully informed of his plans and intentions. It was this policy, as much as his tactical ability, which led to his glittering success as a naval commander.

To those for whom the study of human strength and frailty is more absorbing than the ebb and flow of battle, there was, of course, another great story behind the chronicle of Admiral Viscount Nelson, Duke of Brontë, victor of Copenhagen and Trafalgar. It was the story of his passionate and turbulent love affair with Emma Hamilton. Lady Hamilton was the daughter of a Cheshire blacksmith and the wife of Sir William Hamilton, who was at the Neapolitan Court when Nelson sailed into Naples Bay on 22 September 1798. From that day on, the liaison was the worst-kept secret in the long history of British hypocrisy. Emma, by most accounts, was a somewhat surprising *femme fatale*. She was coarse and loud-mouthed; while a young girl she had become pregnant by one man while the acknowledged mistress of another. She was much given to making dramatic scenes in public, a somewhat disadvantageous characteristic in a woman at any time, but positively disastrous in one pursuing an illicit relationship with a public figure. Yet Nelson developed an obsessive infatuation for this remarkable woman, and ignored all the attempts of his friends and colleagues to warn him of the scandalous concern with which their behaviour was regarded. They indulged in childishly ineffective stratagems designed to conceal their relationship which Nelson to the end protested, ridiculously, was entirely innocent. Emma returned Nelson's passion with a great torrent of flattery and hero-worship, and for him she could do no wrong. When Lady Nelson, after many years, finally tired of her constant humiliation, she demanded that Nelson should choose between his wife and his mistress. His reply was characteristic: 'Take care, Fanny, what you say. I love you sincerely; but I cannot forget my obligations to Lady Hamilton, or speak of her otherwise than with affection and admiration.' Not surprisingly, Lady Nelson left shortly after this uncompromising exchange, and they never lived together again.

This, then, is the story not only of a great sailor, but also of a national hero who was not prepared to adjust either his temperament or his private affairs to the demands of his public position. It is interesting to speculate how he would have fared had he been born into the twentieth century instead of the eighteenth.

Lord Chalfont

1 'The Merest Boy' 1758-87

HORATIO NELSON IS THE AUTHENTIC HERO of British history. His three great victories assured him of his country's gratitude: the manner in which they were won added glory to success. But Nelson was the man to love as well as to admire. He caught public attention by his equal disregard for the traditions of naval warfare and the canons of conventional morality. He excited the people's imagination by both his zest for battle and his bizarre personal life. He inspired the sailors who fought with him, and the feelings he aroused in the fleet spread throughout Great Britain. He believed implicitly in his own destiny, and his death – at the moment when he had extinguished the threat of French invasion for ever – seemed to confirm that each detail of his life was preordained. A purpose could be detected in every previous incident – even the prosaic beginnings in the East Anglian parsonage in 1758.

The victor of Trafalgar – the fifth surviving child of the Reverend Edmund Nelson, Rector of Burnham Thorpe in the county of Norfolk – was born on 29 September 1758. In the Nelson family, the clerical connection was strong. Both of Horatio's grandfathers were in Holy Orders, so were two of his great-uncles, eight of his cousins and two of his brothers. For an eighteenth-century parson with no private income, life was necessarily austere. An inevitably frugal childhood was made even harder by the Rector's unshakeable belief in 'Air, Exercise, Warmth and Cleanliness' and a 'Liberal education: the only antidote against Selfish Cunning, a passion few are exempt from'. The children of the rectory were forbidden to allow their spines to touch the backs of their chairs. Spectacles were prohibited to the weak-eyed Nelson sisters for they were judged a sign of self-indulgence.

Some facts of medical life were acknowledged. Of the eleven children Catherine Nelson had borne in seventeen years, three had died within weeks of their arrival. In consequence, Horatio, like his brothers and sisters, was christened twice – privately within ten days of his birth and publicly when he was a year old. That was no more than a religious precaution and is certainly not evidence of special concern for his infant life and health. But he was a small baby and as he grew, his pale complexion made him look fragile as well as fair. Before he was ten, he began to exhibit both the fearlessness and the apparent need for love and comfort which was so to move the British people thirty years later.

Burnham Thorpe Rectory where young Horatio was taught the virtues of 'Air, Exercise, Worth and Cleanliness' and a 'Liberal education: the only antidote against Selfish Cunning'.

After his death, his biographers began to look for the first signs of courage that took his ships through the enemy lines of battle at Copenhagen, Aboukir Bay and Trafalgar. The earliest example they discovered or invented took place in his ninth year. During a visit to his grandmother he was late returning from a bird-nesting expedition. After hours of searching, he was discovered, calm but exhausted, sitting on a river-bank. Had he, his grandmother inquired, not been driven to distraction by fear? His answer was to be quoted by every newspaper in England after each of his victories: 'I never saw Fear. What is it?'

The meaning of grief he discovered during the winter of 1767 when his mother, Catherine Nelson, died. Little is

The Reverend Edmund
Nelson, Rector of Burnham
Thorpe in the county of
Norfolk and father of
Horatio Nelson.

PREVIOUS PAGES
Commemorative painting
by Nicholas Pocock of ships
in which Nelson served –
Agamemnon (extreme left),
Vanguard (behind
Agamemnon), *Elephant* (left
centre), *Victory* (right).

known of her. Thirty years later when the legend had begun
to grow, Susannah, her eldest daughter, insisted 'Somehow
the Navy must always be interesting to me. I may say that I
sucked it with my mother's milk, for she was quite a heroine
to the sailors.' Nelson himself confided to the world that 'the
thought of former days brings all my mother to my heart,
which shows itself in my eyes'. It rarely showed itself in his
speech or writing. He recorded only one fact about her: 'She
hated the French.'

Yet the legacy that she left her son was crucial to his future
career. For from her side of the family he gained his connection with the Navy and the sea. Catherine Nelson's most
illustrious relation was Sir Robert Walpole, politician,
Prime Minister to George II and brother to her maternal
grandmother. But a closer, less illustrious connection had a
deeper significance in Horatio's life. Catherine's brother,

Catherine Nelson, Horatio's mother. About her, Admiral Nelson recorded only one fact, 'She hated the French'.

Captain Maurice Suckling, was famous, at least in his own family. In 1759 the *Dreadnought*, under his command, together with two other sixty-four-gun ships had engaged a vastly superior French fleet off the West Indies. In the Burnham Thorpe parsonage, Captain Suckling's passage of arms was celebrated every year on its anniversary, 21 October. And it was more than the traditions of the sea which Suckling brought to young Nelson's life. It was the opportunity to join the Navy.

Nelson's formal education began at the Royal Grammar School in Norwich. A few months in an establishment at Downham Market was followed by the completion of his schooling at the Paston School, North Walsham. Of his school days, only a few facts are recorded. Lowered by sheets from a dormitory window, he stole apples, as schoolboys have always stolen apples, but insisted that 'I only took them

17

because every other boy was afraid.' In 1802, Levett Hanson, an un-remembered classmate, provided possible evidence that Horatio had been intellectually precocious: 'Your Lordship,' he wrote, 'though in the second class when I was in the first, was five years my junior.'

But there was neither time nor opportunity for the development of academic talent. Each of his mother's brothers felt under an obligation to their dead sister's sons. William Suckling, an official of the Customs and Navy Office, found an opening for Maurice Nelson in the 'Auditor's Office in the Excise'. Captain Maurice Suckling promised to do as well for another of the parson's boys.

The opportunity came early in Nelson's life. During the Christmas holidays of 1771 Horatio and his brother William read in the local paper that the *Raisonnable* – a ship of sixty-four guns captured from the French in 1758 – was to be re-commissioned as a result of what Nelson himself described as 'the disturbance with Spain relative to Falkland's Islands' – the dispute concerning sovereignty over the windswept South Atlantic colony. The Captain of the *Raisonnable* was to be Maurice Suckling.

The Reverend Edmund Nelson was sick and in the care of West Country relatives. Horatio could not wait for his return: 'Do, brother William, write to my father at Bath and tell him that I should like to go with my uncle Maurice to sea.' The request was passed on. Captain Suckling, with the gift of a place within his power, agreed with a surprised concern for his nephew's welfare. His reply referred to Horatio by the name still used within the family 'What has poor Horace done, who is so weak that he above all the rest should be sent to rough it at sea? But let him come; and the first time we go into action, a cannon-ball may knock off his head and provide for him at once.' Providing for the Nelson boys was, as Suckling knew, all important. Seven had yet to be found places.

There were a few more weeks at school (for after twelve years in an English dock-yard, the *Raisonnable* was not ready for sea) before Edmund Nelson and his sailor son left for London. After a night at Uncle William's house in Kentish Town, Horatio set out alone for Chatham. At first, he could not find his ship. When he was guided to it, he discovered that Captain Suckling was not on board. No one had heard of the twelve-year-old new recruit. It was twenty-four hours before anyone took any notice of him.

18

Captain Maurice Suckling, a portrait painted in 1754 by Thomas Bardwell – five years before his victory over the French in the West Indies and eighteen before his nephew, Horatio Nelson, joined him aboard the *Raisonnable*.

Despite his uncle's foreboding, Nelson's head remained firmly on his shoulders. Not a single cannon ball was aimed at the *Raisonnable* and the war with Spain spluttered out without her firing a single shot. The ship was paid off, but Captain Suckling was given command of the seventy-four-gun *Triumph*, stationed as guardship in the River Thames. His nephew's name was placed in the ship's muster book, but in reality Horatio joined the merchant navy.

A vessel owned by Messrs Hibbert, Purrier and Norton was sailing for the West Indies. Its master, John Rathbone, had served with Suckling in the *Dreadnought* and Nelson was placed in his charge to learn more of the sailor's craft. 'If it did not improve my education', Nelson wrote years later, 'I returned a practical seaman.' But his return to the *Triumph* –

The *Racehorse* and the *Carcass* sail north on their voyage of Arctic discovery. 'Persons under age' were excluded from the expedition yet 'nothing could prevent' Nelson's joining Captain Lutwidge.

first as Captain's Servant then as Midshipman – was not for long. 'By degrees', he wrote of his days on the Thames guard-ship, 'I became confident of myself amongst the rocks and sands, which has many times been of great comfort to me.' But his restless spirit, no matter how willing he was in later life to pay lip-service to the benefits derived from poring over the charts of London River, was not long satisfied with the in-shore routine. The next chance for adventure was not long in coming.

A few weeks before his fifteenth birthday, Nelson heard that two ships, *Racehorse* and *Carcass*, were about to set sail for the Arctic on a voyage of exploration sponsored by the Royal Society. Skeffington Lutwidge, the Captain of *Carcass*, Nelson already knew. 'Persons under age' were excluded from the crews, being adjudged of 'no use' in the desperate weather the expedition expected to meet. 'Yet', said Nelson,

20

'nothing could prevent my using every interest to go with Captain Lutwidge.' He had no doubt that he could 'fill a man's place', so he begged that he 'might be cockswain: which, finding my ardent desire for going with him, Captain L. complied with'.

Inevitably, the expedition – which got within ten degrees of the Pole – was trapped in the ice. It was feared that the ships would have to be abandoned. The plan was to haul the ships' boats across the ice until they could be floated and sailed south. Nelson, to his delight, had been given command of a twelve-man, four-oared cutter, 'fancying I could navigate her better than any other ship'. Having proved his seamanship in July 1773 by the rescue of a party of officers who had been routed by the walrus which they had gratuitously attacked, he prepared to take part in the long haul south. On 8 August, the ships' crews pulled on as much extra clothing as they could wear and remain comparatively agile, and waited for 4 a.m. the following day when the escape was to be made. Suddenly, the wind shifted, the fog that had covered the ice began to disappear and the sound of cracking ice confirmed that the thaw had begun.

No doubt one crew-member would have welcomed the chance to shine that a dash south might have provided. Earlier in the expedition he had exhibited the first signs of the extraordinary ambivalence towards discipline and authority which characterised much of his naval career. The protector of protocol and the defender of the proper order was always prepared to disobey in a good cause. And he knew no better cause than glory.

When there was a gamble between 'laurels and cypresses' he was always willing to risk receiving one in the hope of winning the other. But it was not only life and limb he was prepared to wager. Had his waywardness in battle ended in defeat rather than victory, reputation would have been sacrificed as well. As his reckless independence was invariably crowned with success, he grew to believe that providence expected him to pursue glory as singlemindedly as he pursued the bear on the Arctic ice in 1773.

During the middle watch of one long night during the *Carcass*'s Arctic imprisonment, Nelson and a seaman he had persuaded to accompany him stole away over the ice under the cover of mist and darkness. Hours later, when the fog lifted, two figures were sighted several hundred yards from the ship, facing a huge bear across a narrow crevasse. A signal ordering immediate return was made. The seaman responded. Nelson remained; first firing at the bear, then attempting to club it with the butt of his rifle. Captain Lutwidge, deciding that the hunter was in greater danger than the hunted, ordered a cannon to be fired and the bear lumbered off. With capture obviously impossible, Nelson returned to his ship blandly to explain: 'I wished to kill the bear that I might carry its skin to my father.' If both glory and obedience called, Nelson heard only one voice.

In the autumn of 1773 he heard the call again. The *Seahorse*, under the command of Captain Farmer, sailed for the East Indies in company with the *Salisbury*, the flagship of Admiral Sir Edward Hughes. Nelson, having heard of its imminent departure, asked that he might sail with her for 'nothing less than such a distant voyage could, in the least,

'I wished to kill the bear that I might carry its skin to my father.'

satisfy my desire for maritime knowledge'. First rated as Midshipman, by the spring of 1774 he was re-classified Able Seaman. He 'watched in the foretop; from whence, in time I was placed on the quarter-deck, having in the time I was in this ship visited almost every part of the East Indies'.

He did more than that. He met Thomas Troubridge who was to be his lifelong friend and the recipient of some of his most revealing correspondence. He fell ill with fever and the rest of his life was haunted by its re-appearance. And, for the first time, he believed that he understood his destiny.

In Bombay during December 1775, his condition was so serious that his chances of survival were rated virtually nil. The only hope was an immediate return to England. He was transferred to the *Dolphin* (the ship in which Byron had circumnavigated the globe ten years before) and sailed for London.

The fever itself induced severe depression. When the sickness began to subside, a new depression, the fear that his naval career was over, took over from the old trauma. At times he 'wished himself overboard'; then, one night the 'radiant orb' which, for the next thirty years, was to appear to him in moments of crisis, beckoned him on. From that moment he became sufficiently confident of his own destiny to confide his belief in providence's purpose to his closest friends. By the end of his life, it had enthused the Navy and assured him of victory when victory depended on the devoted confidence of his men. In the summer of 1776, for the first time, 'a sudden glow of patriotism was kindled within me and presented my King and Country as my Patron. My mind exulted the idea. "Well then" I explained "I will be a hero, and confiding in Providence, I will brave every danger."'

The *Dolphin* was paid off on 24 September 1776. Within two days, Nelson – the fever having passed during the last days of the voyage home – was ordered to join the *Worcester*, a sixty-four-gun ship of the line. Uncle Suckling – now Comptroller of the Navy and contemplating a Parliamentary candidature at Portsmouth – had again exercised his highly-developed sense of family duty. The Navy was in need of experienced seamen. The War of American Independence had dragged on for almost a year and France was about to turn from sympathetic neutrality to positive support for the revolution. British merchantmen in Mediterranean waters were to be provided with escorts. Nelson remained 'at sea with convoys until April 2nd 1777 and in very bad weather; but although my age might have been sufficient cause for not entrusting me with a Watch, yet Captain Robinson used to say he felt as easy when I was upon deck as any officer in the ship'.

A week after the convoy duties ended, Nelson took his Lieutenant's examination. A Lieutenant's Certificate was awarded only to officers with six years' sea apprenticeship who were at least twenty years of age. The first requirement Nelson satisfied. Testimonials were provided by the captains under whom he had served. They included the assurance that he could 'splice, knot, reef a sail, etcetera'. The second he did not, for he was still five months from his twentieth birthday. The Captains who conducted the final oral examination either did not know or did not care. Nor did the members of the Board realise that the candidate was the nephew of its President. After Nelson's suitability had been unanimously agreed, the Comptroller of the Navy explained 'I did not want the younker to be favoured. I felt convinced that he would pass a good examination; and you see gentlemen, I have not been disappointed.'

Nelson 'received [his] Commission on the following day for a fine Frigate of 32 guns', the *Lowestoft*, under the command of Captain William Locker, who remained his friend, confidant and correspondent for the rest of his life. Locker had fought under Hawke at Quiberon Bay, and through him Nelson inherited Hawke's views of fighting the French. 'Always lay the Frenchmen close', Locker advised, 'and you will beat him.' Twenty years later, Nelson remembered: 'I have been your scholar; it is you who taught me to board a Frenchman.'

The *Lowestoft*, with eighteen merchantmen in convoy, set sail for the West Indies. Once at Port Royal, the frigate picked up what prizes she could capture. The pursuit of prize-money was most attractive to Nelson when honour and glory were also involved. When an American merchantman overhauled in heavy seas proved difficult to capture, Locker asked (no doubt in part rhetorically), 'Have I no officer who can board a prize?' The Master of the *Lowestoft* volunteered – only to be forestalled by the young Second Lieutenant who announced 'It is my turn now, if I don't come back it is yours.'

In the summer of 1778, a new Commander-in-Chief arrived in the West Indies. Admiral Sir Peter Parker had promised the Comptroller of the Navy that, once in the Caribbean, he would promote young Horatio. By the time he arrived in Port Royal, Suckling was dead. But the promise was still kept and Nelson was moved into the Admiral's flagship, first as Third Lieutenant but within a week becoming First. By the end of the year, he was in command of the *Badger* and 'proceeding to the Mosquito Shore off Honduras'. How much of this phenomenally swift promotion was the result of influence, how much the just reward of merit, it is impossible to know. Certainly Nelson owed (and felt) a debt of gratitude to his uncle – not only for patronage, but for the spirit of service and sacrifice that Suckling had encouraged. 'Had I been near him', Nelson wrote of the Comptroller's death, 'he would have said to me "my boy, I leave you to my country; serve her well, and she'll never desert, but will ultimately reward you."' It was advice to which Nelson was permanently and pathologically sympathetic.

On 11 June 1779 Nelson was promoted Post-Captain, the last competitive rank in the eighteenth-century Navy. After that, promotion was the inevitable result of seniority. If both the war and Nelson lasted long enough, he would become an Admiral. But nothing was certain for sailors. 'I got my rank by a shot killing a Post-Captain', wrote Nelson. 'I most sincerely hope that I shall, when I go, go out of the world the same way.'

The new Post-Captain was given command of the *Hinchingbrooke*. At the moment of Nelson's promotion, the ship was still at sea. While waiting her return, Captain Nelson took charge of the shore batteries which protected Port Royal, Kingston and Spanish Town. Jamaica expected hourly invasion from Haiti or Martinique where the Comte d'Estaign had twenty-five thousand soldiers ready to sail against the British West Indies. Nelson, commanding seven thousand men, supplemented by a few hundred Negro slaves, left 'you in England to judge what a stand we shall make' and wryly warned, in a letter to Locker, 'You must not be surprised to hear of my learning to speak French.'

But the expected invasion did not come and 'In January, 1780, an Expedition being resolved against St Juan [Nelson] was chosen to command the land part of it.' Nelson, never over-modest in the account of his exploits, later described his role: 'I guided my Ship, carried troops in boats one hundred miles up a river which none but the Spaniards since the time of the buccaneers had ever ascended – I made batteries and afterwards fought them, and was a principal cause of our success.'

The expedition's object was the capture of Lake Nicaragua, 'the inland Gibraltar of Spanish America'. From there, they intended to march to the Pacific, 'thus cutting off all communications between north and south'. Two hundred foot soldiers, a hundred of Dalrymple's Loyal Irish with a handful of Marines and Jamaican volunteers were instructed to acquire 'an empire in one part of America, more extensive than that which [England] was on point of losing in another'.

Nelson's orders required him to convey the troops to the mouth of the San Juan river. Prudence should have encouraged Nelson to do no more than his duty and return to Port Royal, there to await the arrival of the *Janus*, the new command he had been promised within days of entering *Hinchingbrooke*'s Captain's cabin. But Nelson possessed neither prudence nor caution. He was unmoved by the uniquely bad portents for the expedition's future.

Most of the seasoned veterans who were supposed to advise and reinforce the invasion turned out to be so sick with fever that they were a liability rather than an asset. The natives who should have acted as pilots and bearers decided that the English were really in search of slaves. Determined not to be the first bondsmen, they disappeared into the jungle. The San Juan river was so low that the sailors had to drag the boats through the shallows and face leeches as well as snakes and mosquitoes.

Yet Nelson insisted on going up-river with the army and led the assault on the first Spanish citadel that the expedition faced, the small (and easily overcome) island of San Bartholomew. It was their single piece of good fortune. No one knew where the forts – which were the principal objective – were situated. When they were finally located, the army prepared for a long and complicated siege – much to the frustration of Nelson who, buoyed up by his success in the earlier skirmish, was all for immediate assault.

Before the siege was over, reinforcements brought with them the news that Captain Nelson must report at once to Port Royal. Had not the orders for return arrived, it is unlikely that Nelson would have survived the expedition. 'In the *Hinchingbrooke*, with a compliment of two hundred men, eighty-seven took to their beds in one night; and of the two hundred, one hundred and forty-five were buried – I believe

Storming a fort during the expedition to Lake Nicaragua. Although ordered to do no more than carry troops to the mouth of the San Juan river, Nelson marched with Dalrymple's loyal Irish in their campaign against 'the inland Gibraltar of Spanish America'.

very few, not more than ten, survived of that ship's crew.' Had Nelson stayed, notoriously susceptible to tropical disease, he would, almost certainly, not have been one of them. As it was, by the time he arrived in Port Royal, the latent fever had taken over. Unable to carry out his duties, he resigned his command in a 'state of health so bad that [he] was obliged to go to England in the *Lion*, Honourable William Corn-wallis, Captain: whose care and attention saved my life'.

Nelson's account of the part he played in the expedition to San Juan was blatantly and characteristically immodest. But Nelson's self-congratulatory accounts of his conduct have one self-redeeming feature – they are invariably true. His frank enjoyment of his own prowess at arms and the success of nearly all his enterprises was to become one of his most

27

CAPT HORATIO NELSON
1781

endearing characteristics, a revelation of the eternal adolescent inside the schoolboy's frame. That would not have been so had his stories been false. Most were as accurate as his account of the expedition to the Mosquito coast. Many were, like that conceited tale, substantiated by other participators. Captain Poulson, who commanded the infantry at San Juan, wrote in his report: 'A light haired boy came to me in a little frigate. In two or three days he displayed himself, and afterwards he directed all the operations – I want words to express the obligation I owe to that gentleman. He was the first on every service night or day.'

Nelson arrived back in England during the autumn of 1780. By early 1781, his health was 'very nearly perfectly restored'. By August he was ready for sea. His new ship, the twenty-eight-gun *Albemarle*, was a captured Frenchman. While waiting for its keel to be cased in copper and its crew to be recruited, Horatio wrote to his brother William, who was determined to become a naval chaplain: 'Fifty pounds where you are', he argued, 'is much more than equal to what you can get at sea. But I know you will please yourself.' His judgment of his brother's persistence proved correct. Faced with renewed pressure, Nelson wrote, a month later, 'as to my opinion whether you will like it, I say as I always did that it is five to one that you will not'. In December he hoped to kill the idea once and for all: 'I hope you have lost all ideas of going to sea, for the more I see of Chaplains of Men-of-War, the more I dread seeing my brother in such a disagreeable station.'

Bad North Sea weather may have jaundiced Nelson's view of the disagreeable station. So may the frustrating task of shepherding an inevitably unruly convoy which 'behaved as all convoys that I ever did see, shamefully ill, parting every day'. At least the *Albemarle*'s Captain had one consolation, his crew – 'not a man or officer in her I would wish to change'. The Admiralty had, almost without precedent, agreed to Nelson's selecting his own ship's company. That he should make such a request was the first example of that interest in seamen as well as seamanship that lay at the heart of Nelson's mystic ability to inspire love and confidence as well as awe and respect. Twenty years later he himself called it 'the Nelson touch'.

When the *Albemarle* arrived in West Indian water, its crew, like the complement of every other fighting ship, hoped for prize-money to supplement their meagre earnings. On 14

Captain Horatio Nelson by John Francis Rigaud, painted between 1777 and 1781 – the year he requested a transfer from North America ('a fine station for making prize money') to the West Indies ('the station of honour').

29

July 1781, the *Harmony*, a Cape Cod fishing schooner, was captured and her master, Nathaniel Carver, required to pilot the *Albemarle* through the unfamiliar waters of Boston Bay. The English man-of-war (whose navigator could do no better than 'imagine we are getting into the gulf stream, by it getting very squally') was desperately in need of Carver's goodwill. It was provided in such generous measure that when the task was finished, Nelson addressed his captive with conscious and flamboyant courtesy: 'You have rendered us, Sir, a very useful service, and it is not the custom of English seamen to be ungrateful. In the name, therefore, and with the approbation of the Officers of this ship, I return your Schooner and with it this Certificate of your good conduct.' Nelson's gesture was both appreciated and reciprocated. Four months later, when the *Albemarle*'s crew had gone eight weeks without fresh food, *Harmony* was sighted again. Sheep, fowl and fresh vegetables were unloaded on to the *Albemarle*'s deck. Only after much argument would Carver accept payment.

Nelson's scurvy-ridden crew went into hospital in Quebec. During the weeks ashore, their Captain developed the first of his sudden, passionate and imprudent attachments. Mary Simpson was sixteen and the daughter of the garrison's Provost-Marshal. After a month's acquaintance, with no certainty that his ardour was welcomed, Nelson announced his intention to resign from the fleet and beg her hand in marriage. Older and wiser colleagues having persuaded him of his folly, he sailed gloomily south, overcome by the melancholy that invariably suffused him when love affairs (or imagined love affairs) ended. Manhattan Island he hated. 'Money', he prophetically wrote, 'is the great object here, nothing else is attended to.'

A squadron of the West Indies Fleet under the command of Admiral Hood had anchored in New York Harbour a week before the *Albemarle* arrived. Never short of nerve, Nelson contrived a first meeting with the Admiral and then, at a second, asked him for 'a better ship on a better station'. His definition of a better station he had made tactlessly plain to Admiral Digby who had welcomed him to North America with the encouraging news that he 'had come to a fine station for making prize money'. The reply had been brusque: 'Yes sir, but the West Indies is the station of honour.'

It was in the hope of service there that Nelson clambered aboard Hood's flagship and made his request. The Officer of the Watch was amazed by the appearance of his master's visitor, 'the merest boy of a captain I ever beheld, dressed in an antique full laced uniform, unpowdered straw coloured hair and a pigtail a foot long'. The Officer of the Watch was Prince William Henry. Twenty-five years after Nelson's death, he was to become King of England.

Nelson and the *Albemarle* were transferred to the West Indies. But the war with France was temporarily ended and there was little opportunity for the pursuit. By 20 June 1783 they were back in Portsmouth, attempting 'to get the wages due to my good fellows' and experiencing discontent attributed to the 'infernal plan of turning men over from ship to ship so that they cannot feel any loyalty to their officers or their officers care two pence about them'.

Peace having broken out, Nelson determined to make a belated and truncated Grand Tour. His education was to be completed by a brief visit to France and the mastery of the French language. The first he did not enjoy. The second he never accomplished. Inevitably, he fell in love and wrote to his surviving uncle in terms which were typically uninhibited – concerning both his feelings and his need for family charity: 'The critical moment in my life has now arrived. Will you, if I should marry, allow me a hundred pounds a year? ... If nothing is done for me, I know not what I have to trust to. Life is not worth living without happiness.'

Before William Suckling could reply, Nelson had returned to London, toying with the idea of standing for Parliament, and demonstrating that however constant and sensible Nelson was about ships and the sea, about women he was simply silly – not because he felt more or meant less than any other infatuated young man, but because the willingness to open his heart about death, honour and glory, which make him the authentic hero of his age, was matched by the habit of describing his emotions with the same absence of reserve.

Professionally, the absence of reserve served him well. In January of 1784 Nelson sought, and obtained, an interview with Lord Howe (by then First Lord of the Admiralty) in the hope of again being given command of a ship. His brother expressed unflattering surprise at the favourable answer he received and was administered a massive rebuke: 'You ask by what interests did I get a ship. I answer, having served with credit was my recommendation to Lord Howe. Anything in reason that I can ask, I am sure of getting from his justice.'

With the discovery that William's importuning could no longer be resisted, he sent the aspiring naval chaplain his grudging agreement: 'Come when you please, I shall be ready to receive you. Bring your canonicals and sermons. Do not bring any Burnham servants. I am pretty well filled with lumber.'

Among the lumber was Lady Hughes, wife of the Admiral commanding the Leeward Islands ('a great clack') and her daughter Rosy. Lady Hughes was more impressed with Nelson than he with her and she saw and recorded 'the Nelson touch' applied to his midshipmen: 'The timid he never rebuked, but always wished to show them he desired nothing of them that he would not instantly do himself. I have known him say "well sir, I am going to race to the mast head and I beg I may meet you there. . . ." After this excellent example, I have seen a timid youth lead another and rehearse the Captain's words.'

Between Nelson and Richard Hughes himself, there grew up a great enmity. Nelson believed the Admiral 'a great ninny'. Hughes, with some justification, believed the Post-Captain to be a trouble-maker. Nelson, although always ready to disobey orders of which he disapproved, was a stickler for discipline and protocol when his instructions were at risk or his dignity in danger. When the *Boreas* was not properly saluted as she sailed into Port Royal, there was an immediate complaint to the Governor. When he arrived at Antigua, he found a frigate flying the broad pennant of a Commodore. 'As her captain was junior to me, I sent to know the reason for her wearing it.' The pennant was flown on the instructions of a Mr Mountray, a retired officer authorised by Admiral Hughes to act as Commander-in-Chief in the absence of a senior British Officer. Nelson was not satisfied. 'You have no right', he told the ship's captain, 'to obey any man who you do not know is authorised to command you.'

Such incidents might have passed off with no more than mutual annoyance had the next occasion of Nelson's inflexibility not had more justification or more serious consequences. As it had both, a pattern of embarrassment and a reputation for intransigence were established. The Navigation Acts were designed to starve the rebellious colonies into submission by preventing trade between them and any other country in the world. Yet Richard Hughes was 'led by the advice of the Islanders to admit the Yankees to a trade; or at least to wink

The frigate *Boreas* off the island of Nevis. The Governor's failure to acknowledge her arrival in Port Royal with a proper salute produced an immediate complaint from Captain Nelson.

at it'. That, Nelson was not prepared to do. The Governor of the Leeward Islands was soon involved, but not on Nelson's side: 'Old respectable officers of high rank, long service and of a certain life are jealous of being dictated to in their duty by young gentlemen whose service and experience do not entitle them to it.' Nelson was unabashed. On his own authority ('being as old as the Prime Minister of England'), he arrested the four American cargo vessels sailing into the island of Nevis. The execution of his duty so enraged the islanders that a civil prosecution for damages was laid against him. For weeks it was impossible for him to go ashore.

For months Nelson and the Board of Admiralty were in anxious correspondence about the Nevis merchants, their threatened prosecution and their demanded damages. But before the matter was resolved, Nelson discovered – or believed he had discovered – a new scandal. It was reported to him that the merchants who victualled the West Indian fleet were defrauding the ships' captains. As always in such matters, Nelson was zealous to the point of fanaticism. He bombarded every senior officer he knew with details of the alleged corruption and began a series of law-suits that pursued him backward and forward across the Atlantic for over four years.

For Nelson and his brother officers, embarrassment piled

33

Prince William Henry
(later to become William IV)
was deeply attached to
Nelson, on whom he saw
the mark of destiny before it
was clear to others.

on embarrassment. Prince William Henry, quickly promoted
to Post-Captain, had returned to the West Indies, and Nelson
was required to 'dance attendance' on the future king. For the
Prince had developed two basic characteristics which were
not to desert him until the day he gave place to the young
Victoria. He was passionately attached to Nelson, on whom
he saw the mark of destiny before it was clear to many others.
And he had a fierce, but capricious, devotion to discipline. It
was, therefore, natural enough that Prince William Henry
should retell to Nelson, with spluttering indignation, a story
of insubordination by two of his officers. Unfortunately for

the young Post-Captain, one, Lieutenant Schonberg, was certain of his innocence and made a formal request to 'Captain Nelson, Senior British Officer on the Station' for a formal court-martial and the chance to clear his name.

Nelson, sympathetic to the sailor but loyal to the Prince, tried to accommodate both and pleased neither. The court-martial was eventually avoided and Schonberg was transferred to Hood's flagship. But Nelson's letter intending to provide a mollifying end to the matter was hardly a model of tact: 'Nothing is wanting to make you the darling of the English Nation but truth. Sorry I am to say, much to the contrary has been dispersed.'

The Schonberg affair was not the last the Admiralty were to hear of Nelson's indiscretions. On 6 April 1787, Seaman Clarke (who served aboard HMS *Rattler* with Wilfred Collingwood, Nelson's lifelong friend) was convicted of desertion. Nelson, Court-Martial President, sentenced the prisoner to death as the law required. Prince William Henry interceded and Nelson gladly granted his plea for clemency: 'The law might not have supposed me guilty of murder, but my feelings would very nearly have been the same.' In his relief, Nelson went to a typical extreme. Clarke was not simply reprieved, he was allowed to leave the service. The Admiralty issued an official reprimand.

Captain Nelson was developing a reputation for being a difficult officer. He was to pay dearly for it during the next five years. On 30 November 1787 he was paid off. England and France were at peace again and awkward officers were not in great demand. Nelson remained on shore and at home until the spring of 1793.

2 'To Glory we Steer' 1787-97

NELSON PREPARED TO FACE the frustration of life ashore with at least one consolation inherited from the hard years in the West Indies. During the days when the merchants of Nevis forced him to remain aboard the *Boreas*, the time passed slowly despite 'the music, dancing, cudgelling etc'. For, a few weeks earlier, Nelson had written to his father with the news that he was visiting 'Miss Parry Herbert and a young widow'. Both were nieces of the President of the Council of Nevis. Mr Herbert was 'very rich and proud . . . with a house open to all strangers'. The single niece had travelled to Nevis on Nelson's frigate. To her widowed cousin, Fanny, she wrote a long description of 'the Captain of the *Boreas* of whom so much has been said', concluding that 'If you, Fanny, had been there, we think you would have made something of him; for you have been in the habit of attending to those odd sort of people.' When the young widow and the odd sort of person met, Nelson was just recovering from an un-reciprocated passion for Mrs Mountray, wife of the retired officer whose Broad Pennant had so annoyed him. Within five weeks of his first meeting with Fanny, Nelson proposed marriage.

Three problems stood in his way. The first was the lady's reluctance – or at least her reluctance to give her immediate consent. The second was the lady's uncle who raised no objection to the match but was loath quickly to lose such an excellent housekeeper. Third, Horatio could not support a wife (particularly a wife who already had a son) in the manner to which Nelson believed his family should be accustomed. The third problem Nelson hoped to resolve by the simple – and for him regular – remedy of banking on family help. Money would eventually come the Nelsons' way from Mr Herbert, and Horatio thought that he 'knew the way to get him to give me the most': that was 'not to appear to want it'. So he wrote once more to Uncle William Suckling, asking 'Who can I apply to but you? Don't disappoint or my heart will break.' Like Mr Herbert, Horatio Nelson was throughout his life a proud man. But it was a partial pride which, in his early years, inevitably deserted him when he had financial favours to ask his family.

On the assumption that the family would provide, Nelson pursued his courtship, entreating the lady to accept his proposal and describing his passion in every letter home. To Mr Suckling he wrote, 'My affection for her is fixed upon that solid basis of esteem and regard that I trust can only increase

PREVIOUS PAGES Nelson boarding the *San Nicholas*, 1797, during the battle of Cape St Vincent, an engraving by A. Reeve. Having captured the frigate, Nelson and his men made a second leap to board the *San Josef*. The *San Nicholas* passed into naval mythology as 'Nelson's patent bridge for boarding first rates'.

LEFT Miniature of Lady Nelson painted by Daniel Orme in 1798 when she was about forty, eleven years after her first meeting with Horatio Nelson on the island of Nevis.

39

by a larger knowledge of her.' To brother William he offered the prophetic opinion, 'I have not the least doubt but that we shall be a happy pair: the fault will be mine if we are not.' To Fanny went an enticingly stern warning that to a young woman must have seemed more romantic than forbidding: 'Duty is the great business of a sea officer. All private considerations must give way to it, no matter how painful.' But usually his messages were simpler. 'Separated from my dearest', he asked, 'what pleasure can I feel?' On 11 March 1787, with Prince William Henry to give the bride away, they were united – if not for life then at least for the long six years that Nelson was to spend ashore.

Life ashore, temporarily quartered with his father in the Burnham Thorpe parsonage, soon palled. He began to bombard the Admiralty with requests for employment. He tried – and failed – to make a personal plea to Lord Chatham and eventually obtained a brief interview with Lord Hood. Its outcome was so unsatisfactory that even the usually importunate Nelson did not knock on Hood's door again for over two years. Certain that there was 'a prejudice at the Admiralty, evidently against me, which I can neither guess at, nor in the least account for', he responded with exactly the sort of behaviour that had caused the original offence – he went over the Admiralty's head.

Prince William Henry (by now created Duke of Clarence) was sympathetic and astonished to learn of the deterioration in Nelson's relations with Lord Hood. Nelson himself remained bewildered about its cause, explaining 'I certainly cannot look on Lord Hood as my friend; but I have the satisfaction of knowing that I never gave his Lordship just cause to be my enemy.' The satisfaction of a job at sea was denied him. The Duke of Clarence spoke to Chatham. The Prime Minister could not or would not help. After two years of bitter frustration, Nelson approached Lord Hood again: 'My wish to be employed is so great, that I trespass on your Lordship's time with a letter. I am sensible I have no great interest to recommend me nor have I had conspicuous opportunities of distinguishing myself. . . .'

Opportunity to distinguish himself was a further two years away. In early 1792 it appeared that Nelson's prospects were permanently gloomy, for the reserve officers' fortunes deteriorated as the prospects of peace improved and William Pitt assured the House of Commons that 'There never was a

Admiral Lord Hood by
L. Abbott. By 1788 Nelson
had so antagonised the
Admiralty that he could not
'look on Lord Hood as a
friend' but claimed he
'never gave his Lordship
cause to be my enemy'.

time when, from the situation of Europe we might more
reasonably expect fifteen years of peace.'

Fortunately for Nelson, Pitt was wrong. On 21 September
1792 France was declared a Republic. A month later, the
Netherlands were overrun, giving the revolutionary government command of the River Scheldt. Within two months,
Britain's susceptibilities had been offended and her trade-
routes threatened. The inevitable response was an expansion

of the Navy. In January 1793 Nelson was able to write: 'After the clouds comes sunshine. The Admiralty so smile upon me, that really I am as much surprised as when they frowned. Lord Chatham made many apologies for not having given me a ship before this time and said that if I chose to take a sixty-four to begin with, I should be appointed to one as soon as she was ready; and whenever it was in his power, I should be removed to a seventy-four.'

On 7 February 1793 Nelson took command of the *Agamemnon*. Four days later, France formally declared war on England. Nelson sailed for Toulon in March with orders to report to Admiral Hood and take part in his blockade of the port. Believing that the people of Toulon ached for the overthrow of the Republic and longed for a chance to declare their allegiance to Louis XVI, Hood determined to invade. Nelson was dispatched to Naples to recruit extra troops. On 12 September he was 'in sight of Mount Vesuvius, which shows a fine light to us in Naples Bay'. As always, his thoughts were divided between the welfare of his sailors and the hope of preferment. 'My poor fellows have not had a morsel of fresh

The capture of Toulon by the army of the Republic. The British underestimated the people's support for the Jacobin cause and were forced to withdraw in such haste that the previously captured French fleet was left intact in the harbour.

Sir John Acton,
by D.E.Ströhling; English
gentleman, Neapolitan Prime
Minister and friend to Sir
William and Lady Hamilton.

meat and vegetables for nearly 19 weeks. . . . We are absolutely sick with fatigue . . . I may have lost an appointment by being sent off; not that I wish to be employed off my ship.'

The journey from Toulon to Naples was more momentous than he could have imagined. In Naples he met King Ferdinand and his Queen, the sister of Marie Antoinette, and found their hatred of the Jacobins infectious. He also met John Acton, English gentleman and Neapolitan Prime Minister, who did his best to cement relations between his native country's Navy and the Court of his adopted nation. Most important of all, Nelson met Sir William Hamilton – His Britannic Majesty's Representative in Naples – and his wife Emma. Their joint influence upon him was to set Nelson on a course on which he was to remain forever. But in 1793 they seemed a passing acquaintance.

By 5 October, after a false alarm and a quick sortie against imaginary attack, Nelson and the Neapolitan troops rejoined Hood's fleet. By the end of the year, Hood's relations with Nelson were restored. The Admiral had become 'certainly the best officer I ever saw. Every order from him is so clear, it is impossible to misunderstand him.' Some of Hood's allies were less certain of his invincibility than was his young Post-Captain. The occupation of Toulon was not a success. A young artillery officer, Napoleon Buonaparte (the Italian 'u' had yet to be expurgated from his name), was leading the revolutionary army towards the coast. The evacuation was hurried and bungled. The plan to burn the captured French fleet failed and eighteen ships were left intact.

The British fell back on Corsica. Nelson was dispatched in advance of the main fleet to find and parley with General Paoli, the Corsican patriot who, it was hoped, would cooperate with the allies in the expulsion of the French. The ageing General's support did not spare the invading English the task of investing and eventually overcoming Corsica's three ancient strongholds. San Fiorenzo, Bastia and Calvi had stood in the path of invasion for a thousand years. In February 1794 San Fiorenzo surrendered before the British Army under General Dundas could attack. At the first sight of Hood's armada, the French had retreated to the fortress of Bastia. General Dundas (and his second-in-command, Lieutenant-Colonel John Moore) told Admiral Hood that immediate attack on that citadel was not possible. Expected reinforcements from Gibraltar had not arrived.

43

LEFT General Paoli, the Corsican patriot who – it was hoped – would co-operate with the allies in the expulsion of the French.
RIGHT Sir John Moore, who died during the retreat from Corunna, was second-in-command of the land forces during the siege of Bastia.

Nelson, having been entrusted with the reconnoitre, was asked his opinion about the vulnerability of the French garrison. His report to Hood was a simple deceit. The attack on Bastia was, to Nelson, a matter of honour which Hood could be persuaded to undertake only if he were misled about the strength of the defending army. Nelson's report was wrong about the size of the garrison, but right about the condition of his ship: 'A thousand men would, to a certainty take Bastia; with 500 and *Agamemnon* I would attempt it. We are really without firing, wine, beef, pork, flour and almost without water. Not a rope, canvas, twine or nail in the Ship. . . . Not a man has slept dry for many months: yet . . . my wish is to be present at the attack.' Hood was convinced.

The operation against Bastia began on 4 April. The building of the two principal batteries took eight days. By mid May – assisted by the eagerly-awaited reinforcements and 'consternation, almost insurrection within the walls' – negotiations for surrender began. On 24 May the fortress fell after seven weeks of siege. Nelson, determined to be elated, confided 'I may truly say that this has been a Naval Expedition' and marched on to the next redoubt, Calvi, in company with General Charles Stuart – a general eager for action and, therefore, much more to his taste. The sailors were again responsible for 'dragging cannon up steep mountains and carrying shot and shell to batteries built, armed and manned under [Nelson's] personal supervision'.

It was hard work. 'All the prevailing disorders' attacked Nelson and in addition to the physical strain he had emotional crosses to bear. 'I am very busy, yet own I am in all my glory. Except with you, I would not be anywhere but where I am', he wrote to Fanny. But he added sadly 'I am well aware that my poor services will not be noticed.' Nelson was smarting from the description of his activities that appeared in Hood's dispatch after the siege of Bastia. A Captain Anthony Hunt had been praised as 'Commander of the batteries', while Nelson was credited simply with 'commanding and directing the seamen, landing guns, mortars and stores'. Nelson chose to be lofty about Hood's error: 'There is nothing like kicking down the ladder a man rises by. Lord Hood and myself were never better friends, nor (although his letter does) did he wish to put me where I never was – in the rear.'

He was not in the rear on 12 July. On the fifth day of the siege of Calvi, an enemy shot struck the ground a few feet in front of him. Fragments of shrapnel and rock struck him in the face. 'I got a little hurt this morning', he wrote to Hood, and reported the following day that he was ready to resume his place in the line of battle: 'My eye is better and I hope not entirely to lose the sight.' Nelson's name never appeared on the casualty list but despite the early optimism of the surgeons, it soon became clear that he had virtually lost the sight of his eye. Despite the intense pain (of what would probably now be described as a totally detached retina), Nelson was philosophical. 'I feel the want of it', he wrote, 'but such is the chance of war; it was within a hair's breadth of taking off my head.'

The siege of Calvi dragged on into the hot summer. Before its surrender on 10 August, Nelson began to feel that, for a second time, his service and sacrifice were being overlooked. 'One hundred and ten days I have been actually engaged at sea and on shore against the enemy', he told Locker, 'I don't know anyone who has done more, and I have had the comfort to be ever *applauded* by my Commander-in-Chief, but never *rewarded*; and what is more mortifying, for services in which I

45

have been slightly wounded, others have been praised, *who at the time were actually in bed*.' But, as always, self-pity and self-confidence mixed and mingled: 'They have not done me justice. But never mind, I'll have a "Gazette" of my own.'

Nelson's final task for Hood was undertaken in September 1794. Within days of Nelson's successful negotiation for victualling facilities in the Venetian ports, the Commander-in-Chief in whose name the deal had been done retired to England. His successor was Vice-Admiral Hotham who, having discovered Nelson's 'enthusiasm for action', dispatched him first to find the disposition of the French fleet, then to Leghorn for a refit of the *Agamemnon* in anticipation of sterner action.

On 10 March 1795, Hotham's fleet, fourteen British and one Neapolitan warship, set sail in search of the French. 'My character', wrote the Captain of the *Agamemnon*, 'and good name are in my own keeping. Life with disgrace is dreadful. A

RIGHT Vice-Admiral Hotham, Hood's successor as Commander-in-Chief of the Mediterranean Fleet. His tactics disappointed Nelson: 'Had I commanded our fleet on the 14th . . . the whole French fleet would have graced my triumph, or I should have been in a confounded scrape.'

LEFT Nelson loses his eye during the siege of Calvi – 'I feel the want of it, but such is the chance of war; it was within a hair's breadth of taking off my head.'

glorious death is to be envied.' The French fleet turned into the wind at the first sight of the British Navy but Hotham's fleet made immediate pursuit.

The *Agamemnon*, far ahead of the rest of Hotham's ships, opened fire on the eighty-gun *Ça Ira* and 'seeing plainly from the situation of the two fleets the impossibility of being supported . . . resolved to fire as soon as I thought we had a certainty of hitting. Scarcely a shot seemed to miss' and, with the French man-of-war 'a perfect wreck', Nelson was about to move against the rest of the French fleet when Hotham ('being much cooler than myself') gave the order to break off the engagement, insisting 'We must be contented. We have done very well.' Nelson felt no obligation to disguise his disapproval. 'Had we taken ten sail, and allowed the eleventh to escape when it had been possible to have got her, I could never have called it well done', he wrote. 'We should have had such a day as, I believe, the annals of England never produced.' To his wife he was even more frank: 'Sure I am, had I commanded our fleet on the 14th, that either the whole French fleet would have graced my triumph, or I should have been in a confounded scrape.'

New opportunities for triumph appeared. Nelson, an experienced infantryman, was sent 'to co-operate with the Austrian General Baron de Vins in the Riviera of Genoa' who hoped to drive the French from the Italian Riviera and gain command of the northern Italian ports.

Nelson left the harbour of San Fiorenzo on 4 July 1795. Three days later he sighted – and was sighted by – the full French fleet. The *Agamemnon* was chased back into San Fiorenzo harbour, from which Hotham (who had done nothing to cover Nelson's escape) sailed out to face the enemy whom he had allowed to escape four months before. Inevitably, some of the English ships outpaced the others. Inevitably Nelson was among them. The early stages of the battle went well: 'In the forenoon we had every prospect of taking every ship in the fleet and at noon it was almost certain we should have had the six rear ships.' But once again Hotham disengaged with the enemy only half beaten. 'The subject', Nelson wrote in his account of the battle, 'is unpleasant and I shall have done with it. I am now co-operating with the Austrian Army, under General de Vins and hope we shall do better there.'

Once again, Nelson was required to intercept merchant-

The *Agamemnon* fires into the *Ça Ira*. Nelson 'resolved to fire as soon as I thought we had a certainty of hitting. Scarcely a shot seemed to miss.'

48

men trading between neutral ports and France. Britain
remained determined to use her maritime power to blockade
France and the countries she had occupied and annexed. But
the dangers of stopping and boarding the wrong merchantmen
– ships with cargoes which the rules of the sea forbade him
to detain – was as real as it had been in the West Indies. The
unhappy events in the Leeward Islands had taught him only
that 'Political courage in an officer abroad is as highly necessary as military courage.' So he frankly admitted to his wife,
'I am acting, not only without the orders of my commander-
in-chief, but in some measure contrary to them. However, I
have not only the support of His Majesty's Minister, both at

49

Turin and Genoa, but a consciousness that I am doing right and proper for the service of our king and country.'

Nelson was always certain that the interest of both king and country were always best interpreted by him. Certainty about the wisdom of his own judgment often produced unattractive doubts about both the competence and the motives of anyone who disagreed with him. Hotham, he told his old friend Captain Collingwood, '*entre nous* has no political courage whatsoever and is alarmed at the mention of any strong measure'. Although de Vins was 'a good man and I verily believe a good General', he was also the heir to an unhappy tradition: 'War is their trade, and peace is ruin to them; therefore we cannot expect that they should have any wish to finish the war.'

On 19 January 1796 Nelson at last met a commander-in-chief whose loyalty and courage commanded his complete affection and respect. Sir John Jervis was sixty-three. Behind him was a lifetime of naval service marked by conspicuous bravery and a deep devotion to rigorous discipline. He was the sort of commander Nelson needed, not least because the campaign in the Italian Riviera had, like all Nelson's previous campaigns, ended in less than total victory.

When the land battle eventually came, 'the Austrians', according to Nelson, 'did not stand firm. The French, half naked, were determined to conquer or die. General de Vins, from ill health he says, gave up command in the middle of the battle and from that moment not a soldier stayed at his post.' On 4 December Nelson was on his way to Leghorn to refit, overcome by the melancholy that invariably followed an unsuccessful encounter. 'The campaign is finished by the defeat of the Austrians, and the French are in possession of Vado Bay. My ship and ships' company are worn out, but the folks at home do not feel for us.'

The fleet which he joined in San Fiorenzo Bay was in an altogether different condition; 'in excellent order', according to Collingwood, 'well provided with everything, in which our Admiral, Sir John Jervis, takes wonderful pains, and the consequence is we are remarkably healthy after being 28 weeks at sea'. Nelson's spirits were immediately improved by the offer of a choice of new ships and the promise that he would soon be promoted to Rear-Admiral. Both of the new ships were refused, but Nelson had no doubt that when the Mediterranean fleet sailed out for action, he and his *Agamem-*

non would sail with them. But for some months Nelson had to resume the pursuit and harassment of French shipping sailing into the Italian ports. The revolutionary army, sweeping through the Ligurian Hills, had been promised the spoils from 'the most fertile plains in the world'. Nelson had to be content with the prospect of future glory and the immediate pleasure of being appointed Commodore. In June 1796 he transferred his flag to the seventy-four-gun *Captain*.

In northern Italy, Bonaparte had proved irresistible. Leghorn, weeks earlier the refuge for British ships during refit, was under French occupation. After mounting a blockade on his recent haven, Nelson was ordered to supervise the evacuation of Bastia, the town which, two years before, had been one of the victories of the Corsican campaign. British hopes in the Mediterranean were dwindling. Nelson bitterly recalled that 'When we quitted Toulon we endeavoured to reconcile ourselves to Corsica; now we are content with Elba – such things are.' Even that was not the end of the humiliation. Elba too had to be surrendered and, on his way to evacuate the garrison, Nelson learned of Admiral Man's decision to ignore his orders to stand and fight and retreat from Gibraltar harbour.

The evacuation, Nelson wrote to Fanny, was 'not a fighting mission'. That was not how it turned out. On 15 December 1796, aboard the *Minerve* and accompanied by the *Blanche* under his command, he put to sea. Five days later two Spanish frigates – the *Santa Sabina* and the *Ceres* – were sighted off Cartagena. A strict interpretation of his orders would have resulted in Nelson's avoiding action and making best speed for Elba. That was not Nelson's way, as his own account of the incident makes plain:

When I hailed the Don [Jacobo Stuart, great-grandson of James II] and told him 'This is an English frigate' and demanded his surrender, or I would fire into him, his answer was noble, and such as became the illustrious family from which he is descended – 'This is a Spanish frigate and you may begin as soon as you please' I have no idea of a sharper or closer battle.

During the battle, the *Minerve* so suffered that her captain and crew 'very nearly escaped visiting a Spanish prison'. The *Santa Sabina* was boarded, but the Spaniards repulsed their attacks so successfully that 'Two lieutenants and a number of men were taken.' Nelson ended the action a good deal less

The Battle of Cape St Vincent

The battle of Cape St Vincent, fought on
14 February 1797, was the first occasion when
Nelson earned the reputation which gave him
his place in history. By turning his ship out of
line in order to prevent the junction between two
portions of the Spanish fleet, a sudden and
spontaneous act for which he had no authority,
he entirely defeated the Spanish movement, and
made victory for the British possible. As
Admiral Jervis conceded: 'Commodore Nelson
. . . contributed very much to the fortune of the
day.' Nelson went on to capture two Spanish
ships – the *San Nicholas* and the *San Josef*.

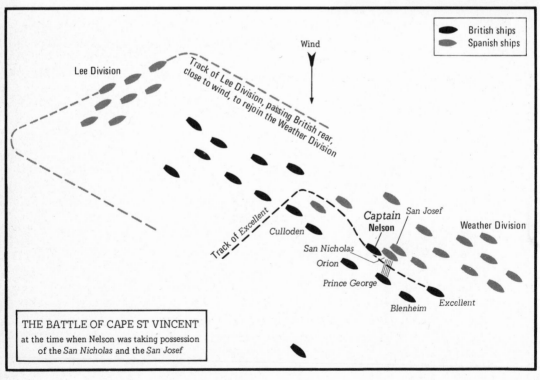

Wind

Lee Division

Track of Lee Division, passing British rear,
close to wind, to rejoin the Weather Division

British ships
Spanish ships

Track of Excellent

Culloden

San Nicholas

Orion

Prince George

Captain
Nelson

San Josef

Weather Division

Blenheim

Excellent

THE BATTLE OF CAPE ST VINCENT
at the time when Nelson was taking possession
of the *San Nicholas* and the *San Josef*

LEFT 'Nelson's patent bridge for boarding first rates' – the *Captain* captures the *San Nicholas* and the *San Josef*.

BELOW Commodore Nelson receiving the sword of the dying Spanish Admiral on the quarterdeck of the captured *San Josef*.

equipped to carry out his primary mission, the evacuation of Elba – a task Nelson further postponed while he negotiated for an exchange of prisoners in a flowery correspondence with Don Miguel Gaston, Captain General of the Department of Cartagena, and Admiral Don Juan Marino: 'Sir: the fortune of war put *La Sabina* into my possession after she had been most gallantly defended; the fickle Dame returned her to you with some of my officers and men in her.' But before the exchange could be completed, Nelson felt forced to sail on to Elba. The allied troops were evacuated on 29 January and Nelson returned to Gibraltar to collect the Spaniards' prisoners. One was Lieutenant Culverhouse; the other, Lieutenant Hardy who, once reunited with the fleet was hardly away from Nelson's side until the day in 1805 when the victor of Trafalgar died in his arms.

Elba evacuated and the prisoners returned, Nelson left Gibraltar to join Jervis's fleet off Cadiz. Nelson had barely left port when two Spanish ships were sighted. Colonel John Drinkwater aboard the *Minerve* was congratulating Lieutenant Hardy on his release when he heard a cry 'man overboard'. The soldier ran to the stern-windows 'to see if anything could be observed of the unfortunate man'. He had 'scarcely reached them before we noticed the lowering of the jolly-boat, in which was my late neighbour, Hardy, with a party of sailors; and before many seconds had elapsed the current of the straits (which runs strongly to the eastward) had carried the jolly-boat astern of the frigate, towards the Spanish ships'.

The missing sailor was given up for lost. 'The jolly-boat's crew pulled might and main to regain the frigate, but apparently made little progress against the current.' By now Nelson was in the stern: 'By God, I'll not lose Hardy: back the mizzen topsail.' As a result, the *Minerve* was allowed to float with the current towards the jolly-boat whose crew, 'seeing this spirited manœuvre, naturally redoubled their exertions to rejoin the frigate'. To the landsmen on board the *Minerve* Colonel Drinkwater wrote, 'An action now appeared to be inevitable.' But the bewildered Spanish, baffled by the sight of an English frigate being carried towards them by the tide, 'afforded time for the *Minerve* to drop down to the jolly-boat to take out Hardy and the crew'. The battered British ships escaped. More important, the fact-turned-legend of Nelson's devotion to his crew continued to grow.

On 13 February 1797 the *Minerve* rejoined Hood's fleet.

A lookout in Nelson's topmast had sighted Spanish sail making hard for Cadiz, but the intelligence added nothing to Jervis's battle plan. The Admiral already knew of the Spaniards' whereabouts and guessed their intention. On 14 February, with Nelson restored to the command of the *Captain*, the enemy were sighted again off the Portuguese headland of Cape St Vincent, still 150 miles north-west of Cadiz. The British (fifteen sail of the line) were heavily out-numbered. John Jervis's First Captain identified twenty-seven Spaniards before he was told 'Enough of that Sir, if there are fifty sail I will go through them.' The Spaniards ('looking like Beachy Head in fog') were undermanned and strung out in loose formation. It was the sort of situation in which Jervis's special talents were particularly valuable. He planned to sail through their open line and, keeping them scattered and divided, attack the Spaniards section by section. It was a strategy Nelson copied in battle after battle.

Jervis's plan was precise. The British ships would pass through the Spanish line with all speed, thus reducing the risk of the enemy's closing its ranks and annihilating the allied fleet as it failed to batter its way through the re-formed Spanish formation. Nelson, in the rear of the fleet, suddenly realised that the Spanish line was tightening with such speed that the *Culloden* might reach the gap too late to keep it open. Without orders, Nelson pulled out of the line and overtook the *Diadem* and the *Excellent* and engaged seven Spaniards. For over an hour the *Captain* and the *Culloden* held out alone. Then the Spaniards' fire was diverted by the *Blenheim*. Nelson had broken specific orders. He had also behaved with spectacular heroism. Nelson virtually offered his ship as the lever which would keep the gap in the Spanish line open and allow the rest of the fleet to penetrate their line of battle. As the fire was concentrated on the *Captain* a second time, Jervis ordered the *Excellent* to provide support. Together, though severely damaged, Nelson and Collingwood's ships fought their way back to the fleet.

That was, however, only the beginning of the day for Nelson. Soon the *San Nicholas* was alongside. Nelson wrote his own account of the engagement:

At this time, the *Captain* having lost her fore-top mast, not a sail, shroud of rope standing; the wheel shot away and incapable of further service in the line or in chase, I directed Captain Miller to put the helm a-starboard, and calling for the boarders ordered

The battle of Cape
St Vincent – the end of
the engagement.

them to board. . . . The first man who jumped into the enemy's
mizzen-chains was Captain Berry, late my First Lieutenant. He
was supported from our spirit-sail-yard; and a soldier of the 69th
Regiment having broke the upper quarter gallery window, jumped
in, followed by myself and others – Having pushed on the quarter-
deck, I found Captain Berry in possession of the poop and the
Spanish Ensign hauling down.

But the day's work was still not over. 'The *San Josef* at this
moment fired muskets and pistols from Admiral's galley on
us.' Nelson decided to attempt capture of the second, larger

ship. 'Having placed sentinels at the different ladders and ordered Captain Miller to push more men into the *San Nicholas*, I directed my brave fellows to board the first rate, which was done in a moment. When I got into the main-chains, a Spanish officer came upon the quarter-deck rail without arms and said that the ship had surrendered.' For Nelson there were two moments of triumph to come: 'A Spanish captain with bended knee' presented his sword and announced the formal surrender of the *San Josef*. The second tribute was from his own men who, in memory of Nelson's leap to the *San Nicholas* and from that frigate to the mighty *San Josef*, provided their own immortal description of the double capture: 'Nelson's patent bridge for boarding first rates.'

The *Minerve* had been so damaged in the day's combat that Nelson took command of the *Irresistible*. But before his flag was hoisted on the new command, Nelson had to face Jervis and discover whether the Admiral's admiration of valour would outweigh his insistence on discipline in his assessments of the *Minerve*'s conduct. Aboard the *Victory*, Nelson was relieved to recount, 'The Admiral received me on the quarter-deck, and having embraced me, said he could not sufficiently thank me, and used every kind expression which could not fail to make me happy.' But the happiness was to be short-lived. 'The attainment of public honours, and the ambition to be distinguished above his fellows', Colonel Drinkwater had noted, 'were his master passions.' That passion was a result of Cape St Vincent, gratified within the fleet. But national acclaim was still elusive.

Only one subordinate officer received immediate public praise – Robert Calder, Jervis's Fleet Captain. That, Nelson believed, was the establishment's punishment for his disobeying orders during the morning's engagement. It was Calder who had urged Jervis to reprimand Nelson for leaving the planned battle-line and sailing to the support of the *Culloden* – on the improbable principle that Nelson's behaviour might constitute a precedent. Admiral Jervis conceded that orders had been disobeyed: 'It certainly was so, and if ever you commit such a breach of your orders, I will forgive you also.' However, the forgiveness was probably not complete. Nelson was convinced that his initiative – Calder would have called it insubordination – was the cause of his omission from Jervis's dispatches when he later read their contents. One sentence seemed an ironic reference to the special part the *Minerve* had played: 'The correct conduct of every officer and man made it impossible to distinguish one more than others.'

England, in desperate need of a victory, acclaimed the victor of Cape St Vincent with an enthusiasm that neither Parliament nor people had felt for fifty years. Jervis became Earl St Vincent and subsidiary honours were awarded to his captains. Nelson was considered for a baronetcy, but loudly expressed himself for a less illustrious decoration and had, eventually, to be content with the Order of the Bath. As unofficial accounts of the battle reached England, fame and praise began to multiply.

From the West Indies, Lady Parker, wife of Nelson's old West Indies Commander, was explicit: 'Your conduct on the memorable February 14th, a proud day for Old England, is above all praise – long may you live, my dear Nelson, an ornament to your country and your profession.' From 3 February 1797 Nelson ornamented old England in the rank of Admiral. The order – which had been gazetted before the battle – reached him as the British fleet set sail for Lagos and the battered Spaniards made for Cadiz.

3
Laurel
or Cypress?
1797-8

IN APRIL 1797, NELSON, the junior flag officer of the British Navy, was given command of the Mediterranean in-shore squadron – a post which by its nature was virtually independent of the Commander-in-Chief. Once again, Nelson was charged with the mounting of a commercial blockade, but at least on this occasion, its rigid application was the wish – indeed the instruction – of his superiors. John Jervis, now Earl St Vincent, hoped that by stopping all supplies from entering Cadiz, he could force the Spanish fleet to sea.

Nelson was always chafed by the inactivity of a blockade. After a few stationary weeks, he detached his ship – on his own initiative and authority – and sailed to the assistance of General de Burgh who was completing the withdrawal from Elba in which Nelson had been engaged a few months before. The last of the allied ships having been shepherded into Gibraltar, Nelson resumed command of his squadron on 24 May and hoisted his flag on the *Theseus*. The new flagship – which Captain Miller had sailed to Cadiz while Nelson was guarding the Elba convoy – was described to St Vincent as 'an abomination'. No doubt Nelson, always a strict disciplinarian when the rigours of discipline applied to others – agreed. For, among the crew of the *Theseus*, there were potential mutineers.

Discontent, the product of low pay, poor food and harsh discipline, had rumbled in the Navy through the autumn of 1796 and on into the spring of 1797. At Spithead the mutineers made a list of their demands and, to the surprise of the fleet, they were conceded by the Admiralty. But at the Nore the mutineers were less precise. In fact their leader, Richard Parker, seemed anxious only to ensure that the Admiralty would suffer a second humiliation – much to the concern of 'the Seamen of Spithead' who wrote a reproving message to 'their brethren at the Nore' explaining that 'It is with the utmost concern that we see several ships' companies continue in a state of disaffection and illegal proceedings, notwithstanding every demand made by our Brethren in Lord Bridport's fleet have been most graciously granted . . . we have wrote these lines whilst unmooring, and preparing to go out to sea to face our enemies.'

What the Spithead mutineers had achieved gave hope to many desperate sailors. The undercurrent of rebellion was soon running throughout the rest of the Navy. St Vincent, whose fleet was no exception to the general contagion, decided

PREVIOUS PAGES The battle of the Nile: ten o'clock on the evening of 1 August 1798. At the height of the engagement, *L'Orient* blows up.

OPPOSITE Richard Parker, on behalf of the mutineers at the Nore, hands a list of grievances to Admiral Buckner. The Admiral St Vincent believed it his duty to 'direct these animals from the damnable doctrine' of rebellion and sedition.

The Life of Seamen in Nelson's Day

Ordinary seamen made up about two-thirds of a ship's company. They were either recruited as volunteers attracted by the bounties offered, or rounded up by press gangs, which usually happened only in time of war. One of the chief causes of complaint was the low rate of pay – until 1797 able seamen were paid only twenty-four shillings a month. The money was not handed over until the ship was paid off, usually after years of service. After the mutinies of 1797 pay was raised by five shillings and sixpence a month. Shore leave was forbidden for fear of desertion. Discipline was maintained by flogging and sometimes men were beaten to death for severe offences. Although life on board was frequently savage, depending to a great extent on the captain, who exercised great powers of discipline on his ship, it was often equally harsh for the poor on land as well.

BELOW The press gang in action. James Gillray's 'The Liberty of the Subject'.
RIGHT The main deck of a man of war, by T. Sutherland.

BELOW RIGHT 'Firing a Cannon on a British Battleship' by Thomas Richardson.

All True-Blue
BRITISH HEARTS OF OAK

Who are able, and no doubt willing, to serve their Good

KING and COUNTRY
ON BOARD OF
His Majesty's SHIPS,

Are hereby invited to repair to the Roundabout Tavern, near New Crane, Wapping, where they will find

Lieut. JAMES AYSCOUGH,
Of the BELLONA,

Who still keeps open his right real Senior, General and Royal,

Portsmouth Rendezvous,

For the Entertainment and Reception of such

Gallant SEAMEN

Who are proud to serve on board of the Ships now lying at

Portsmouth, Plymouth, Chatham and Sheerness,
Under the COMMAND of

Vice-Admiral Geary, Rear-Admiral George Lord Edgcumbe, and Commodore Hill; viz. The

Centaur	74	Prince of Wales	74	Bell-Isle	70	Portland	54
St. Antonio	74	Defence	74	Buckingham	64	Minerva	32
Bellona	74	Temeraire	74	Achilles	ditto	Rainbow	44
Ajax	74	Fame	—	Yarmouth	—	Cerberus	28
Arrogant	74	Prudent	74	Rippon	—	Mercury	20
Hero	74	Ramallies	ditto	Firm	64	Garland	24
Cornwall	ditto	Albion	—	Augusta	—	King's Fisher,	16

With a Number of Frigates and Sloops at the above Ports.

Lieut. Ayscough will be damn'd happy to shake Hands with any of his old Ship-mates in particular, or their jolly Friends in general.—Keep it up, my Boys!—Twenty may play as well as one.

Able Seamen will receive Three Pounds Bounty, and Ordinary Seamen Two Pounds, with Conduct-Money, and their Chests, Bedding, &c. sent Carriage free.

N. B. For the Encouragement of DISCOVERING Seamen, that they may be impressed, a REWARD of TWO POUNDS will be given for Able, and THIRTY SHILLINGS for Ordinary Seamen.

Success to His Majesty's NAVY! With Health and Limbs to the Jolly Tars of Old England---JAMES AYSCOUGH

GOD SAVE THE KING.

Printed by R. HILTON, in WELLCLOSE-SQUARE

that the antidote was hard work, strict discipline and improved living standards. Each night his ship carried on 'the most active desultory war against the port and town of Cadiz to *divert the animals* from those damnable doctrines which letters from England have produced'.

The formula that St Vincent had prescribed was exactly the remedy Nelson would have chosen to apply. It worked so well that on 15 June, the Admiral Commanding the In-Shore Squadron was able to write home: 'A few nights ago a paper was dropped on the quarter-deck of which this is a copy:—"Success attend Admiral Nelson! God bless Captain Miller! We thank them for the officers they have placed over us. We are happy and comfortable and will shed every drop of blood in our veins to support them, and the name of *Theseus* shall be immortalised as high as the *Captain*'s SHIPS COMPANY."' 'The Nelson touch', a strange combination of courage and concern, had begun to influence the conduct of the Navy.

Nelson was not the only admiral of his day with spectacular victories to his credit. Nor was he the only one to believe that life at sea was intolerably harsh and that the press gang was necessary only because too many officers refused to create conditions afloat that free men would willingly endure. But he had the special gift of communicating his feelings to his sailors. Although they knew that he would have been 'happy to command a ship' against 'the Nore scoundrels', they also knew that he believed they were 'a neglected set . . . when peace comes, shamefully treated'. All his emotions were on permanent display. He talked constantly of love and hope, and made no secret of the special role in which he believed destiny had cast him.

The blockade of Cadiz, with frequent but desultory bombardment, continued throughout the spring of 1797. As always, Nelson fretted for action and despised those who avoided it.

We are looking at the ladies walking the walls and Mall [he wrote home], and know of the ridicule they made of their sea officers. Thirty sail are now perfectly ready, and, the first east wind, I expect the Ships from the Mediterranean, which will make them forty sail of the Line. We are now twenty; some of our Ships being always obliged to be absent for water, provisions etc. . . . We in the advance are, night and day, prepared for battle: our friends in England need not fear the event.

St Vincent, sharing his subordinate's impatience, decided

67

Nelson blockades Cadiz. 'We in the advance are, night and day, prepared for battle: our friends in England need not fear the event.'

on a major bombardment of Cadiz on the night of 3 July, hopeful that the Spanish fleet would be forced to choose between sailing out to fight and subduing the people of the town who, it was rumoured, had grown resentful at the pounding they were required to endure in protection of the fleet. Nelson commanded the operation and described it in the *Sketch* of his life which he prepared as the draft of a biography:

My personal courage was more conspicuous than at any other period of my life. . . . I was boarded in my barge with its common crew of ten men, Cockswain, Captain Fremantle, and myself by the Commander of the Gunboats. The Spanish barge rowed twenty-six oars, besides officers, thirty in the whole, this was a service hand to hand with swords in which my Cockswain, John

68

Sykes (now no more) saved twice my life. Eighteen of the Spaniards being killed and several wounded, we succeeded in taking their Commander.

The bombardments, great and small, failed completely to divert the mutineers' attention from mutiny. On 5 July, while a bombardment was actually taking place, four mutinous sailors from the *St George* were tried, convicted and sentenced to death. The mutineers asked for five days to prepare for death but their request was denied (St Vincent feared that 'they would have hatched five hundred treasons') and a hanging was planned for the following morning. The next day was Sunday, so for reasons related to Christian scruples the pious Vice-Admiral Thompson 'presumed to censure the execution on the Sabbath, in a public letter'. St Vincent 'insisted on his being removed from the Fleet immediately'. Nelson, of course, agreed. His sympathy was reserved for worthy, loyal sailors. He also wrote a public letter to St Vincent, 'Had it been Christmas Day instead of Sunday, I would have executed them.'

The people of Cadiz did not turn on the Spanish Navy, and the Spanish fleet did not put to sea. St Vincent, riding out his impatience in the *Victory*, learned that a treasure-ship, *El Principe d'Asturias*, was anchored in Teneriffe. Nelson was ordered in pursuit of this subsidiary prize with the strict injunction 'Having performed your mission you are to make the best of your way back to join me.' Nelson's response was his usual commitment to total victory or absolute failure, with the invariable emphasis on the former: 'Ten hours shall either make me a conqueror or defeat me. We shall get hold of something, if there is anything moving on the face of the waters.'

Nelson sailed for the Teneriffe port of Santa Cruz with a fleet of eight ships. His plan was for the three frigates under his command to sail into the Santa Cruz Bay at night and land a shore party between the forts on the north-east headland and the town. The invaders would then capture the batteries and send an ultimatum to the Governor. That plan failed. On the night of the attack, wind and current were too strong to allow the frigates close to shore before daybreak. Surprise being impossible, Nelson's four ships of the line bombarded the fortress in the hope of creating a diversion. The bombardment did no more than alert the garrison. Nelson abandoned the attempt and determined to take personal command of the next landing-party himself.

At the beginning of every battle, a combination of fatalism and realism prompted Nelson to consider the prospect of death. At Teneriffe, faced with his sailor stepson who insisted on joining the landing-party, he asked a simple (if unavailing) question: 'If we should both fall, Josiah, what would become of your poor mother?' His dispatch to St Vincent contemplates the same fate. But it was written in the grand Nelson manner and expressed emotions which were invariably felt (and usually expressed) before a battle: the imminent choice between death and glory, the nation's obligation to care for a hero's dependants: 'Your partiality will give me credit that all has hitherto been done which was possible, but without effect. This right, I, humble as I am, command the whole, destined to land under the batteries of the Town and tomorrow my head will probably be crowned with either laurel or cypress. I have only to recommend Josiah Nisbet to you and my country.'

On the evening before the assault, Nelson dined aboard the *Seahorse*. Captain Fremantle had recently married and his wife was aboard ship. She noted in her diary that the sailors talked as if 'the taking of this place seemed an easy and almost sure thing' and 'went to bed . . . apprehending no danger to Fremantle'.

The landing boats left the parent ships at eleven o'clock. It took over two hours, rowing against the tide, to approach the shore. At 1.30 a.m. the Spanish opened fire, holing many boats before they reached the shore. Nelson and Fremantle both scrambled out on to the harbour mole, the agreed landing-point. Advance was impossible. Every sailor who attempted it – including Admiral Nelson – was killed or wounded.

Within minutes of the landing, a piece of grapeshot smashed Nelson's right elbow. Lying in the sand, he told his stepson: 'I am a dead man.' Josiah, who half believed his stepfather's prognosis, dragged him into the bottom of a long-boat, covered the shattered arm with his hat (as the sight of blood was making the Admiral feel faint) and began to bandage the wound. As Josiah began to row away from the mole, Nelson began to recover. The *Fox*, he noticed, was hit and sinking. The long-boat, he insisted, must pull over and take survivors on board. After half an hour, all who could be rescued were on board and the long-boat rowed on. Alongside

OPPOSITE Teneriff: '1797 July 25, Admiral Nelson. Compound fracture of right arm by musket ball passing through a little above the elbow . . . the arm was immediately amputated.'

70

Theseus Aug: 16th 1797,

My Dear Sir,

Irejoice at living once more in Sight of Your Flag, and with your permission will come on board the Ville de Paris & pay you my respects. If the Emerald has Joined, You know my wishes, a left handed Admiral will never again be considered as useful therefore the sooner I get to a very humble cottage the better and make room for a better Man to serve the State but whatever be my lot Believe Me with the most sincere affection Your Most faithful

Horatio Nelson

Turn over

Nelson's first left-handed
letter addressed to Earl
St Vincent from Santa Cruz.

the *Seahorse*, the wounded were about to board when Nelson noticed the ship's name. Unless the wound received immediate treatment, Josiah told him, it might be fatal. 'Then I will die', Nelson replied. 'I would rather suffer death than alarm Mrs Fremantle by her seeing me in this state, and when I can give her no tidings of her husband.'

The long-boat pulled on to the *Theseus* which Nelson insisted on boarding without assistance – 'Let me alone! I have my legs left and one arm. Tell the surgeon to make haste and get his instruments. I know I must lose my right arm, so the sooner it is off the better.' That was also the opinion of the ship's surgeon, who wrote in his medical journal: '1797 July 25. Admiral Nelson. Compound fracture of right arm by musket ball passing through a little above the elbow, an artery divided: the arm was immediately amputated and opium afterwards given.' Four days later, 'The stump looked well. No bad symptoms whatever occurred. The sore reduced to the size of a shilling. In perfect health. One of the ligatures not come away.'

The attack on Teneriffe had ended in complete disaster. After Nelson's evacuation, Captain Troubridge and a small force struggled forward. With more nerve than logic, he 'sent a Sergeant with two Gentlemen of the Town, to summon the citadel' but by daybreak (with a force which consisted of 'about 80 marines, 80 pike-men and 180 small-arm Seamen'), he concluded 'the Sergeant was shot on his way, as I heard nothing of him afterwards'. Faced by a large force of advancing Spanish troops, he hoisted a flag of truce. The Spanish Governor sent him food and lent him boats for the evacuation of the British.

The battle over, Nelson began the slow, left-handed construction of the obligatory letters. For Don Antonio Gutierrez, the Commandant General of the Canary Islands, there was 'most sincere thanks for . . . humanity in favour of our wounded men in your power'. For St Vincent there was a message of abject misery: 'I am become a burden to my friends and useless to my country . . . you will perceive my anxiety for the promotion of my son-in-law, Josiah Nisbet. When I leave your command, I become dead to the World; I go hence, and am no more seen . . . the Boy is under obligation to me, but he repaid me by bringing me from the Mole of Santa Cruz. I hope you will be able to give me a frigate to convey my carcase to England.'

73

The North Parade, Bath, by Thomas Malton.

The mood continued. On 16 August his squadron rejoined the fleet but, Nelson told St Vincent, 'A left handed Admiral will never again be considered as useful, therefore the sooner I get a very humble cottage the better.' The Commander-in-Chief replied with a message that was neither original nor totally tactful: 'Mortals cannot command success. You and your companions have certainly deserved it, by the greatest degree of heroism and perseverance that was ever exhibited. Give my love to Mrs Fremantle. I will salute her and bow to your stump tomorrow.' The courtesies done, Nelson and Captain Fremantle (who had suffered only a slight wound) set sail for England. St Vincent's accompanying dispatch hoped that 'both of them will live to render important service to their King and Country'.

Nelson arrived at Spithead on 1 September, home in England for the first time in four years. By 3 September he was in Bath, his arrival greeted by the *Bath Journal*:

Arrived at Bath – Lady Ann Mahon, Sir John Snow, Sir William Addington, Admiral Sir Horatio Nelson. . . . The Rear Admiral who was received at Portsmouth on the 1st with a universal greeting, reached Bath on Sunday evening in good health and spirits,

74

to the great joy of his Lady and Venerable Father, and gratification of every admirer of British Valour. The brave Admiral certainly owes his country no service; he has signalized himself in as exemplary a manner as any hero that graces the Naval Annals of this country, and with the loss of a right arm – it might have been supposed that he would sit quietly down 'with all his budding honours thick about him'. But it is said that he eagerly longs to repair to that station on which his name has been the pride of the British fleet and the terror of the enemy.

Nelson's honour and reputation had survived Teneriffe intact. His physical condition was, however, a great deal worse than the *Theseus*'s surgeon had originally supposed. Assured that only time could produce a complete cure, Nelson attempted to live a normal, if painful life. A visit to London included not only a visit to a surgeon, but daily visits to the Admiralty (both to remind them of his continued existence and to complete the formalities involved in the receipt of a pension) and attendance at an investiture where he was dubbed Knight of the Bath and was delighted to be told 'Your country has a claim for a bit more of you.'

It seemed unlikely that Nelson would be able to respond. The stump of his amputated arm did not heal, but grew increasingly painful and swollen. The ligature which had been applied aboard the *Theseus* had not come away and Nelson – muttering 'anything better than ingratitude' – dragged himself to Norwich (to accept the Freedom of the City) and to the Guildhall (to receive a gold casket) in the belief that a second operation would be necessary. But there was some good news. The *Foudroyant*, of eighty-six guns, was to be launched in January. When commissioned the following month, she was to be Nelson's. The prospect of the sea seemed to have an almost magical effect. Within days of receiving the news, he slept, for the first time in three months, without drugs. When his dressing was changed the following morning, the ligature was no longer fast to the wound and the real recovery had begun. On 8 December he wrote to Berry, his 'right hand' and Fleet Captain, 'If you mean to marry, I would recommend your doing it speedily . . . for I am well and you may expect to be called for every hour.' For the Vicar of St George's, Hanover Square, he had a request: 'An officer desires to return thanks to Almighty God for his perfect recovery from a severe wound, and also for many mercies bestowed upon him.'

On 21 December 1797, the *Foudroyant*'s construction being far behind schedule, Nelson was given the *Vanguard* as his flagship. While that was in final preparation for its new occupant, Nelson made a brief return to Bath. Letters awaiting him there told the story of Captain John Williamson, court-martialled for his conduct during the victory of Camperdown. Nelson (who on hearing news of the victory confessed 'I would give this other arm to be with Duncan at this moment') took a severe view of Williamson's misconduct and a critical one of the court-martial's lenient sentence. 'Upon the general question, that if a man does not do his utmost in time of Action, I think but one punishment ought to be inflicted. . . . I would have every man believe, I shall only take my chance of being shot by the Enemy, but if I do not take that chance, I am certain of being shot by my friends.' Nelson's view on the severity of punishment changed from incident to incident, and he was invariably more ferocious when talking about draconian punishment than when faced with the prospect of inflicting it.

Four months later, Nelson and the *Vanguard* rejoined Admiral Lord St Vincent's Mediterranean fleet. His arrival, St Vincent wrote, 'has given me new life. . . . His presence in the Mediterranean is so very essential that I mean to put the *Orion* and *Alexander* under his command, with the addition of three or four frigates and to send him away . . . to ascertain the real object of the preparations making by the French.'

Those real objectives could be determined only by constant patrol. On 4 May Nelson was in Gibraltar. By the 6th he was off Toulon. On the 17th a French frigate was captured and the discovery made that Bonaparte's fleet was about to set sail. On the morning of 21 May, 'exhilarated beyond description', he was off the coast of Corsica. The exhilaration did not last the day. A sudden gale demasted the *Vanguard* and dispersed the squadron. Nelson tried to be philosophical.

I ought not to call what has happened to the *Vanguard* by the name of accident [he wrote to his wife]. I believe firmly that it was the Almighty's Goodness to check my consummate vanity. I hope it has made me a better Officer as I feel confident it has made me a better man. I kiss with all humility the rod. Figure yourself this proud, conceited man, when the sun rose on Monday morning, his ship dismasted, his fleet dispersed and himself in such distress that the merest frigate out of France would have been a very unwelcome guest.

But like most of Nelson's moral musings, he ended up on the side of the Providence for it 'pleased Almighty God to bring us to a safe Port, where . . . the *Vanguard* will in two days get to sea again, as an English Man of War'.

Four days in Sardinia did not, however, prove a complete cure for the squadron's difficulties. On 27 May the three ships of the line were ready for sea, but the frigates – 'the eyes of the fleet' – were missing, separated from the rest of the squadron by the gale and attempting a *rendezvous* with their commander in the belief that he had taken his broken ship to Gibraltar. Their captains could hardly be blamed for losing position. At the height of the storm on 20 May, Bonaparte had left Toulon and, unnoticed, had passed within a few hundred yards of the British fleet.

On 7 June, Nelson received both reinforcements and new orders. Twelve ships of the line were added to his command (including the *Culloden* captained by Troubridge and the *Leander* under Hardy) and he was instructed to use his 'utmost endeavours to take, burn, sink or destroy' the French and 'to open a correspondence with His Majesty's Ministers at every court in Italy, at Vienna and Constantinople, and the different Consuls on the coasts of the seas you are to operate in'. From Naples he sought and obtained friendly neutrality. Sir William Hamilton supplied both victuals and pilots and began a lively correspondence with his old friend. 'My distress for frigates is extreme', Nelson told him. 'I cannot help myself and nobody will help me. But thank God, I am not apt to feel difficulties. Pray, present my best respects to Lady Hamilton. Tell her I hope to be presented to her crowned with laurel or cypress.'

Nelson, without frigates for reconnaissance, was left to do little better than speculate about French intentions. To the First Lord of the Admiralty he explained, 'If they pass Sicily, I shall believe they are going on their scheme of possessing Alexandria and getting troops to India.' Troubridge then brought news from Naples that Malta was the most likely objective. By the time Nelson had passed through the Straits of Messina, Malta had fallen and Bonaparte's armada had loaded the Knights' treasure on *L'Orient* and sailed away. The next objective must, Nelson deduced, be either Corfu or Egypt. Hardy was given command of the fast *Mutine* and sent ahead with urgent dispatches for George Baldwin, the British Consul at Alexandria. On 28 June Nelson arrived in

Aboukir Bay hoping to find the French or a friendly welcome. There was neither.

Three years later Nelson could not bring himself to forgive Baldwin for his absence when he was needed to take the British squadron into the harbour.

I should have been off Alexandria when the French fleet arrived, and most assuredly the Army could not have landed in the complete order it did, had an action taken place on the first of July, which . . . it would have done had the Turks received me as a friend instead of an enemy, for the answer I received was that neither English nor French should enter the port of Alexandria. And I believe if you had been there to explain between me and the Turkish Government that I should have remained a few days to get some water and refreshments.

As it was, finding neither Bonaparte nor anchorage, he again 'stretched the Fleet over the coast of Asia' and grew increasingly concerned about his failure to find the French.

An explanation, he felt, must be sent to St Vincent. Despite the advice of Captain Ball of the *Alexander* who 'recommended a friend never to make a defence before he is accused of error', Nelson decided to forestall the inevitable criticism. He should have had more trust in St Vincent. When Admiral Sir John Orde complained to the Admiralty that 'Sir Horatio Nelson, a junior officer, and just arrived from England, is detached from the Fleet in which we serve' and admitted that he could not 'conceal from your Lordships how much I feel hurt', he was sent home.

On 19 July, Nelson's squadron anchored off Syracuse as ignorant of Bonaparte's whereabouts as when he had left St Vincent. Three days later he left, watered and re-provisioned with copious thanks and another promise to 'return crowned with laurel or covered with cypress'. On 28 July Troubridge was detached from the squadron off southern Greece and sent to find news. For the first time in the whole operation, there was hard evidence of Bonaparte's intentions. A month earlier, the French fleet had been sighted south of Crete. Nelson had guessed right. The destination was Alexandria. The British had arrived too early and left too soon.

It took Nelson four days to reach Alexandria. At 2.45 on the afternoon of 1 August, Hardy sighted the French fleet. It was the rejuvenating climax to months of frustration. One of Nelson's captains could 'not recollect to have felt so utterly hopeless or out of spirits, as when we sat down to dinner,

Bonaparte captures Malta. The treasure of the Knights of Malta having been loaded in *L'Orient*, the French fleet sailed east to Aboukir Bay.

judge then what a change took place when, as the cloth was
being removed, the officer of the watch hastily came in, saying – "Sir, a signal is just now made that the enemy is in
Aboukir Bay, and moored in line of battle."'

Admiral Brueys, the Commander-in-Chief of the French
fleet, was confident that if the British came, they would be
defeated. Aboukir Bay was shallow and at its entrance were
shoals and breakwaters. The French anchored in a crescent

79

formation, close to the shoals in the shallow water behind Bequier Island on which batteries had been mounted, and covered their exposed flank with frigates and gunboats. The combination of such a secure position and a fleet superior to the British in both numbers and fire power made the French feel impregnable. When the British fleet appeared on the horizon, it seemed inconceivable that they would attack, if at all, until next day.

Admiral Brueys, confident that there would be no immediate attack, made virtually no preparations for battle. Shore parties were not recalled. Even when it seemed that the English might be mad enough to risk a night engagement, he decided that it was safe to engage the enemy at anchor. The attack, he reasoned, could come only from the seaward side, as Nelson possessed no charts of the shoals and would not risk sailing close to the shore. So his strongest ship (*L'Orient* with 120 guns) went into the centre of the line. His eighty-gun men-of-war protected the rear.

The assumption that Nelson could not know the exact position of the shoals was correct. The conclusion that he would not risk sailing through them was not. Captain Berry recalled that 'It instantly struck his eager penetrating mind, that where there was room for an Enemy's ship to swing, there was room for one of ours to anchor.' The gamble paid off. He concentrated his attack on the French van, choosing to escape the sandbanks by sailing close to the enemy. Only one ship foundered on the shoals.

The British formed a line ahead and astern of the *Vanguard*. At 6.28 p.m., Foley in the *Goliath* steered for the anchor-cable of *Le Guerrier*, the leading enemy ship, and passed unscathed between its stern and the low water off Bequier Island. The *Zealous* and the *Theseus* followed Foley to an inshore position. The *Orion* and the *Audacious* passed between *Le Conquerant* and *Le Guerrier*. Within twelve minutes of the opening shot being fired, *Le Guerrier* was dismasted. The French had been so confident that attack must come from the sea, that guns on the landward side of the ships were not prepared for firing. When it became clear that Nelson intended to brave the shoals and attack from an inshore position, there was mess furniture and baggage to be shifted before the larboard guns could be cut loose and primed.

Nelson anchored the *Vanguard* on Brueys's seaward side

RIGHT John Jervis, Admiral Lord St Vincent. He accepted that Nelson's conduct at the battle from which he took his title was a breach of discipline – 'and if you ever commit such a breach of your orders I will forgive you also'.

BELOW The battle of Cape St Vincent. Without orders, Nelson pushed the *Captain* out of the line of battle, overtook the *Diadem* and the *Excellent* and engaged seven Spaniards.

The Battle of the Nile

Nelson's victory at the Nile on 1 August 1798 brought him immediate fame and popularity. He virtually destroyed the enemy fleet – of the seventeen French ships, thirteen were burned, sunk, driven ashore or captured. As for the British, although they had heavy casualties, not a single ship was damaged irreparably. Nelson was hardly boasting when he said after the battle 'Victory is not a name strong enough for such a scene.'

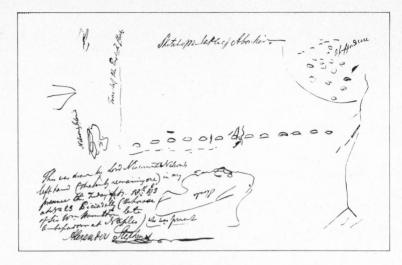

ABOVE Nelson's sketch of the inshore approach drawn after the battle.
OPPOSITE ABOVE The battle of the Nile by Nicholas Pocock. Nelson risked foundering in the shoals, and attacked the enemy fleet from the inshore position.

OPPOSITE BELOW Nelson coming up on deck to see the last minutes of the *L'Orient*, by Daniel Orme. A silver fork, part of the treasure stolen from the Knights of Malta, landed on the *Alexander*'s deck. Captain Berry sent it to Nelson.

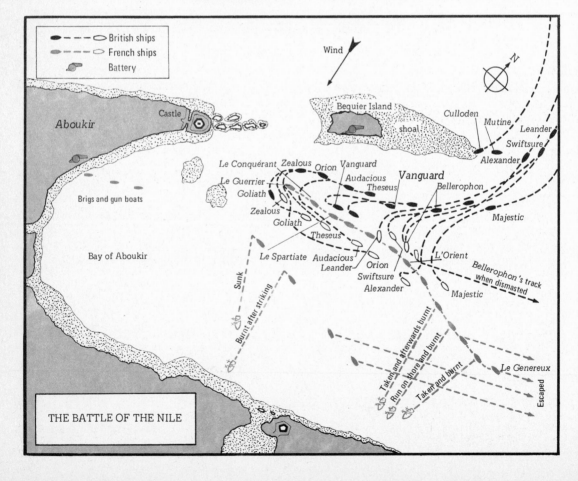

THE BATTLE OF THE NILE

ABOVE The blowing up of the *L'Orient,* by George Arnold.

LEFT The Nile medal.

Admiral Brueys d'Aigailliers, Commander of the French fleet at Aboukir Bay. He was so certain that Nelson would not risk an inshore attack that guns on the landward side of his ships were not prepared for firing.

and opened fire on *Le Spartiate*. It surrendered after two hours of bombardment, the fifth French ship to submit. Two more surrendered during the next hour. *L'Orient*, the treasure-ship that St Vincent had sought for so long, caught fire at nine o'clock. At ten, it exploded, taking to the bottom of Aboukir Bay the gold collected by Bonaparte in Switzerland and Rome to pay for his Egyptian expedition, the precious relics stolen from the Knights of Malta and the body of Brueys who had died from wounds. The explosion was heard ten miles away. It carried a silver dining-fork on to the deck of the *Alexander*. Captain Berry kept it to send to Nelson.

After the explosion, Captain Berry noted 'an awful pause and death-like silence for about three minutes'. But the battle was not over; it continued until three o'clock the next morning with the *Alexander*, *Swiftsure* and *Leander* anchored at the centre of the French line, pounding into the enemy men-of-war. Two French ships of the line and two frigates survived the battle intact. In the English fleet, the *Bellerophon* was almost completely destroyed and the *Majestic* was severely damaged. Forty-nine men died in the *Bellerophon*, fifty in the

85

Majestic; the overall British casualties were little more than a sixth of the French. Captain Troubridge, aboard the beached *Culloden*, sent his crew to help repair the damage and tend the dead. For the second time in his career he had watched, inactive, as other captains assailed the French. In June 1794 he had been a prisoner aboard a French ship, eventually captured by Lord Howe. In August 1798 he was stuck on a sandbank in Aboukir Bay, acting as a light-ship, to warn other captains to avoid the same fate.

The British casualty list included 'Sir Horatio Nelson K.B., Rear Admiral of the Blue . . . wounded on the forehead; over the right eye; the Cranium bare for more than an inch; the wound three inches long.' At 8.30 p.m. – about two hours after the battle began – he had been hit by a piece of shrapnel. As he fell he cried to Berry, his Fleet Captain, 'I am killed; remember me to my wife.' By the time Doctor Jefferson, the *Vanguard*'s surgeon reached him he had grown more sanguine about his prospects and insisted, although his pain was intense, 'No, I will take my turn with my brave fellows.' The flap of flesh detached by the shrapnel had fallen over his 'bright' eye and given, for a moment, the impression of blindness. Once it had been stitched back in place, Nelson began to draft a dispatch. The battle was only two hours old and still had five to run, but the message to St Vincent began: 'Victory is not a name strong enough for such a scene.'

On the day after the battle, Nelson's exhausted fleet (on the *Theseus*, 'as soon as they had hove our sheet anchor up, they dropped under the capstanbars and were asleep, in a moment') gave thanks for victory. A second act of worship followed on 3 August. Under the inspiration of Captain James Saumarez, the fleet passed a resolution:

The Captains of the Squadron under the Orders of Rear Admiral Sir Horatio Nelson K.B., desirous of testifying the high sense they entertain of his prompt decision and intrepid conduct in the Attack on the French Fleet, in Bequier Road, off the Nile, 1st August 1798, request his acceptance of a Sword; and as a further proof of their esteem and regard, hope that he will permit his Portrait to be taken, and hung up in the room belonging to the Egyptian Club, now established in commemoration of that glorious day.

In the evening, the final dispatch was written:

My Lord, Almighty God has blessed his Majesty's Arms in the late Battle, by a Great Victory over the Fleet of the Enemy, whom

86

Nelson and his officers give
prayers of thanks – 'I had
the happiness to command a
band of brothers.'

I attacked at sunset on the 1st of August, off the mouth of the Nile.
The Enemy were moored in a strong Line of Battle for defending
the entrance of the Bay . . . flank'd by numerous Gun-Boats, four
Frigates and a Battery of Guns and Mortars on an Island in their
Van; but nothing could withstand the Squadron your Lordship
did me the honour to place under my command. Their high state
of discipline is well known to you, and with the judgement of the
Captains, together with their valour, and that of the Officers and
Men of every description, it was absolutely irresistible. Could
anything from my pen add to the character of the Captains I would
write it with pleasure, but that is impossible. . . .

A contemporary cartoon (by H.Humphreys of St James Square) shows Nelson's annihilation of the French fleet.

Two sets of dispatches were prepared. One was to be carried by Berry and Thompson in the *Leander* to St Vincent. Capel and Hoste in the *Mutine* carried the news of victory to Naples. Capel gave the joyous message to Sir William and Lady Hamilton and sailed on to England. Berry and Thompson were delayed. *Le Genereux*, a rare survivor of Aboukir Bay, captured them on 18 August. When they eventually reached England, the news had already arrived. Nile captains were the heroes of the hour. Instead of courts-martial for the loss of their ship, both were knighted.

For Nelson there were gifts and honours – £10,000 from the East India Company, a peerage from the King of England. The dukedom of Bronte from the King of the Two Sicilies and 'the invaluable approbation of the great, the immortal Earl Howe, an honour the most flattering a Sea-Officer could receive'. His reply to the 'Great Master of Naval tactics and bravery' contained an account of the engagement, more revealing of Nelson's character than of battle's progress:

88

I had the happiness to command a Band of Brothers; therefore, night was to my advantage. Each knew his duty, and I was sure each would feel for a French ship. By attacking the Enemy's van and centre, the wind blowing directly along their line, I was enabled to throw what force I pleased on a few ships. This plan my friends readily conceived by the signals, (for which we are principally, if not entirely, indebted to your Lordship) and we always kept a superior force to the Enemy. At twenty-eight minutes past six, the sun in the horizon, the firing commenced. At five minutes past ten, when *L'Orient* blew up, having burnt seventy minutes, the six van ships had surrendered. I then pressed further towards the Rear; and had it pleased God that I had not been wounded and stone blind, there cannot be a doubt but that every ship would have been in our possession. But here let it not be supposed, that any officer is to blame. No; on my honour, I am satisfied each did his very best.

4 'Naples is a Dangerous Place' 1798-1800

'THE HERO OF THE NILE' pulled into Naples harbour on the evening of 22 September 1798 with a head which was 'splitting – splitting – splitting'. His reception would have been an ordeal for a less exhausted man. The King of Naples was on hand to greet his 'Deliverer and Preserver' and while Ferdinand performed the role of principal idolator, the Hamiltons led the chorus of adulation: 'Alongside came my honoured friends: the scene in the boat was terribly affecting; up flew her ladyship, and exclaiming "Oh God, is it possible" she fell into my arm more dead than alive. Tears, however, soon set matters to rights.'

Nelson had not seen the Hamiltons for five years, but he quickly re-established his old relationship – a deep affection for them both and a passionate (though at the time, still platonic) attachment to Emma Hamilton's company. In 1799 Lady Hamilton was still a friend about whom letters could be written home to Lady Nelson: 'I hope some day to have the pleasure of introducing you to Lady Hamilton, she is one of the very best women in the world. How few could have made the turn she has. She is an honour to her sex and a proof that a reputation may be regained.'

Not everyone was so certain that Lady Hamilton's social rehabilitation was complete. Captain Josiah Nisbet had publicly expressed what an increasing number of English sailors were thinking when, too drunk to be afraid, he had pointed to Emma and his stepfather and shouted 'That woman is ruining that man.' One thing was, however, beyond doubt. Despite the special status Emma enjoyed in Naples as confidante of Queen Maria Carolina and principal hostess in the Court, no one had forgotten her origins. There was disagreement whether or not her reputation had been regained, but unanimous agreement that it had been lost.

Emma Hamilton was born in 1762, the daughter of a Cheshire blacksmith. In her teens she left the village of Neston to find what London had to offer to a girl with great confidence and few scruples and eventually became the permanent mistress of Sir Harry Fetherstonehaugh. While under his protection, she became pregnant, but her patron was not the father of the child. Dispatched home to Cheshire by her affronted protector, she returned to London and transferred her favours to Sir Charles Greville. From him she obtained two priceless gifts – education in the ways of polite society and an introduction to Greville's uncle, William Hamilton.

PREVIOUS PAGES
A view of Naples by Alexandre Dunovy.

OPPOSITE Admiral Nelson with Nile decorations. Painted by Francis Abbot at Greenwich during the winter of 1797 to 1798.

92

Detractors suggested that the nephew gambled his mistress away or sold her to his uncle. How she passed from hand to hand is uncertain. But the move was made and a second, more difficult, transition also accomplished. Sir William Hamilton, the widower and financial beneficiary of a wealthy heiress, translated her from paramour to wife.

Emma's attraction for Horatio Nelson was only partly physical. Certainly she possessed a powerful, if unconventional, beauty which was sometimes obscured by the coarseness of her conduct and character. Women were particularly severe in their judgment. A Mrs Trench thought her 'bold, forward, coarse, assuming and vain', and added that 'Her figure is colossal, but excepting her big feet, which are hideous, well shaped.' Yet Mrs Trench conceded that 'She resembles the bust of Ariadne; the shape of all her features is fine, as is the form of her head, and particularly her ears . . . her eyes light blue, with a brown spot in one which, though a defect, takes nothing away from her beauty of expression.'

Nelson's affection – which changed swiftly into infatuation – had a simple origin. She produced the sort of voluble, public, unabashed hero-worship on which he thrived. As she planned the festivities to mark his fortieth birthday, Nelson's letters home contained childishly gleeful accounts of her devotions: 'The preparations of Lady Hamilton for celebrating . . . are enough to fill me with vanity. Every ribbon, every button has "Nelson" etc. The whole service is marked "H.N. Glorious 1st of August!" Songs and Sonnetti are numerous beyond what I ever could deserve.' One of the songs was an extra verse to *God Save the King* dedicated to the victory at Aboukir Bay. Nelson sent his wife a copy as he knew she would 'sing it with pleasure' and assured her that 'Good Lady H. preserves all the papers as the highest treat for you.'

Although Nelson wallowed in the adulation of the Neapolitan Court, he was eager to exchange the celebration of old victories for the prospect of new. The French had occupied almost all Italy. Nelson could contemplate, and advise, only one response. King Ferdinand must declare war on Napoleon and his new Republics and march on Rome. In October 1799, Nelson's arguments were reinforced by General Mack, sent by the Austrians to command the Neapolitan army. Nelson was sure what was best for Naples: 'The Ministry, except for Acton, are for putting off the evil day, when it will come with destruction. War at this moment can only save these

Kingdoms', he wrote to St Vincent and added, no doubt to the surprise and embarrassment of the old Admiral, 'I am writing opposite Lady Hamilton, therefore you will not be surprised at the glorious jumble of this letter. Were your Lordship in my place, I must doubt if you could write so well; our hearts and our heads must be all in a flutter. Naples is a dangerous place, and we must keep clear of it.'

Queen Maria Carolina, sister to Marie Antoinette and, according to Bonaparte, 'the only man in Naples', was also anxious for action. At her insistence a Neapolitan army thirty-thousand strong was prepared to march. On 23 November 1798 it was on its way to Rome, and Nelson's squadron, with four thousand soldiers on board, sailed to capture Leghorn and cut the French line of communication. Nelson, despite his earlier anxiety for battle, feared that the campaign would be lost as the hoped-for support from the Austrian army did not come. 'If Mack is defeated, in 14 days this country is lost', he wrote, 'for the Emperor has not yet moved his army and Naples has not the power of resisting the enemy.' When the inevitable defeat came, the army retreated like a routed rabble. Nelson remained unrepentant about the desirability of the campaign. His idea had been right; its execution by the Neapolitan army had been disastrous – 'The officers did not lose much honour, for God knows they had not much to lose . . . but they lost all they had.'

Nelson's devotion was to the Court, not the people of Naples. Having been instrumental in provoking a French attack, he felt that loyalty required him to do no more than safeguard the life and property of the King's coterie. King Ferdinand and family, the Actons and the Hamiltons were loaded into the *Vanguard* along with royal treasure that was thought to be worth no less than two and a half million pounds sterling. On 23 December they sailed for Palermo. They arrived after three storm-tossed days which were so unpleasant that Sir William Hamilton loaded his pistols in preparation for shooting himself as soon as the ship began to sink, rather than 'die with the guggle-guggle-guggle of salt water in his throat'. Poise and dignity were recovered in time for the landing: 'At 9 a.m. His Majesty went on shore and was received with the loudest acclamations of apparent joy.'

Relief at having, at least, saved the royal family from Bonaparte was soon replaced by the chagrin that Nelson always felt at the least suspicion of suggested slight or possible

LEFT Emma
Hamilton. Nelson's
favourite portrait,
it always hung in
his cabin when
he was at sea.

ABOVE Nelson. These two pastel portraits by Heinrich Schmidt were
commissioned in Dresden in 1800 while Nelson and Emma
Hamilton were returning to London overland across Europe.

ABOVE Palermo, where Nelson landed the Sicilian Royal Family and Court after their flight from Naples.

OPPOSITE Sir Sidney Smith who was given command of the British fleet in the Levant. Nelson found it 'impossible – to serve under a junior officer'.

humiliation. The flamboyant Sir Sidney Smith had been sent to the Levant with orders to command the British Navy in the area and to assume virtual ambassadorial powers. Commodore Smith was, accordingly, entitled to act independently of Admiral Nelson. Indeed it might be thought that in eastern Mediterranean waters, Smith was in command and Nelson's duty was to accept his orders. That was not a situation that Nelson would willingly accept. On the last day of 1798, Nelson wrote to St Vincent:

I do feel, for I am a man, that it is impossible for me to serve in these Seas with a Squadron under a junior officer:— could I have thought it! – and from Earl Spencer! Never, never was I so astonished as your letter made me. As soon as I get hold of Troubridge, I shall send him to Egypt, to destroy the Ships in Alexandria. If it can be done, Troubridge will do it. The Swedish Knight [Nelson's denigratory name for Smith] writes to Sir William Hamilton, that he shall go to Egypt, and take Captain

98

Hood and his Squadron under his command. The Knight forgets the respect due to his superior Officer: he has no orders from you to take my ships away from my command, but it is all of a piece. Is it to be borne? Pray grant me permission to retire, and I hope the *Vanguard* will be allowed to convey me and my friends, Sir William and Lady Hamilton to England.

As usual, St Vincent's sympathies were with Nelson. The roles were reversed. 'Employ Sir Sidney Smith in any manner you think proper. Knowing your magnanimity I am sure that you will mortify him as little as possible, consistently with what is due to the great characters senior to him on the List, and his superiors in every sense of the word.'

Although professional relationships were easily clarified, private ones were not. Josiah Nisbet was not behaving in a way of which his stepfather approved. The first letter that Lady Nelson received in 1799 was deeply disturbing: 'I wish I could say much to your and my satisfaction about Josiah, but I am sorry to say and with real grief that he has nothing good about him and must sooner or later be broke.' Captain Nisbet was drinking heavily, but not withstanding

100

that, on 12 February was given command of the *Thalia*. Nelson noticed a slight redemption in his character and wrote to Josiah's mother to explain the reason: 'The improvement made in Josiah by Lady Hamilton is wonderful; your obligations and mine are infinite on that score.'

In fact, Nelson was beginning to show all the signs of total infatuation. He hated Palermo, but longed to stay if Lady Hamilton were there. His ills he attributed to other causes. His blessings he inevitably attributed to her. And in the midst of this emotional turmoil, a further complication arose. Lady Nelson was agitating to join him in Sicily. An old friend wrote in sorrow from England: 'I cannot help again repeating my sincere regret at your continuation in the Mediterranean. . . . Your valuable better half writes to you. She is in good health, but very uneasy and anxious, which is not to be wondered at. . . . She bids me say, that unless you return home in a few months, she will join the Standard at Naples.' Nelson was having none of that. On 10 April 1799 he wrote home: 'You would by February, have seen how unpleasant it would have been had you followed any advice which carried you from

England to a wandering sailor. I could, if you had come, only struck my flag and carried you back again, for it would have been impossible to set up an establishment in either Naples or Palermo.'

Naples had capitulated to the French in early 1799. The Parthenopian Republic which replaced the old kingdom had, like other Bonapartist creations in Italy, the support of both the commercial middle classes and the minor nobility. The Church, however, remained fearful of the French. Cardinal Fabrizio Ruffo hoped and plotted for a restoration. If an uprising were to be led by him, it would be a peasants' revolt. It began in Calabria. Landing on the beach at La Catona without money or arms, he raised a band of fanatical support and began to rage through southern Italy. Nelson responded joyously. Troubridge was sent at once to blockade the Bay of Naples and provide whatever assistance he could. He was immediately successful, capturing both Procida and Ischia, the islands which commanded the western entrance to the Gulf of Naples, and awarding summary punishment to royalist deserters. His view of the Neapolitan army did not differ from Nelson's: 'I desired the General and all his cowardly gang to get out of a British man-of-war. We want people to fight; he does not come under that description. I told him plainly that his King will never do well until he has hanged half his officers.'

Ruffo's success was not the only setback Bonaparte received. A combined Russian and Turkish force captured Corfu. General Charles Stuart and two English regiments from Minorca occupied Messina. The pressure on the Jacobins in southern Italy was building up, but the Bourbons in Sicily were still neither secure in Palermo nor ready to return to their old capital. Their security was further threatened by the news that a French fleet had left Brest and was sailing for Malta and Alexandria in the hope of joining the Spanish fleet on the way. Nelson decided that he must put to sea to meet them, although he knew that 'If I go, I risk and more than risk, Sicily and what is now safe on the Continent.' Nelson and the French fleet did not meet: nor did the Bonapartist navy join with the Spaniards who remained at Cartagena. So Nelson returned to Palermo and the Naples blockade. Twice more he left Palermo in search of the enemy. 'I consider the best defence for his Sicilian Majesty is to place myself along-side the French'. On 21 June – the French still not in sight –

Cardinal Fabrizio Ruffo, minister of Ferdinand IV of Sicily, who led the successful revolt against the French.

he sailed again for Naples in his new flagship, the *Foudroyant*.

His decision to return to Naples was certainly reckless, for it effectively prevented a quick union with Lord Keith (St Vincent's successor as Commander-in-Chief) at Minorca and the establishment of a single British fleet large enough to face any armada the enemy could muster. Undoubtedly the sudden change of plan was, in part, attributable to the basic need for certainty that influenced all that Nelson did. 'To fight is nothing', he told Hamilton as he sailed from Sicily, 'but to be continually on the stretch for news and events of the greatest importance is what I find my shattered carcase very unequal to.' But there was more to it than that. Cardinal

Ruffo – fearing the combined enemy fleet and disgusted by the excesses of his army – was negotiating peace with the Naples Jacobins. That was unacceptable to Queen Maria Carolina whose views on the Jacobins atrophied at the moment her sister had been arrested on the road to Varennes. The Queen told Emma Hamilton that there would be no agreement with the rebels. Emma told Horatio that he must sail from his strategic position off Maritimo for Naples. He left 'full of grief and anxiety'. He hoped that the expedition would 'finish the war' and 'give a sprig of laurel to your affectionate friend Nelson'.

As Nelson sailed for Naples, he learned that Ruffo had negotiated a three-week armistice with the Jacobins during which they, according to the agreement, would evacuate the castles of Nuovo and Uovo with full military honours and the provision of transport for their baggage and lumber. The arrangement was unacceptable to Nelson. There could be neither an armistice nor a treaty with rebels, though a brief truce was permissible with the French garrison in the castle of St Elmo. He decided, therefore, that a joint declaration should be signed by Ruffo and himself giving the French three hours for evacuation after which they would be taken prisoner 'without the stipulation of their being prisoners of war'. The Jacobins could receive no favours as 'No power on earth has a right to stand between their gracious king and them; they must instantly throw themselves on the clemency of their sovereign, for no other terms will be allowed them, nor will the French be allowed even to name them in any Capitulation.'

When Nelson sailed into Naples Bay, he discovered that matters had gone too far to make his stern plans immediately practical. Flags of truce flew over Uovo, Nuovo and St Elmo. Ruffo, Captain Edward Foote (temporarily in command of the *Seahorse*) and the Russian and Turkish plenipotentiaries had signed an agreement with General Meyean which Nelson regarded as more of a capitulation than an armistice. Foote, he decided, had erred, 'being imposed upon by that worthless fellow Ruffo'. The Cardinal must agree to unconditional surrender. A document for his signature was carried to him by Captains Troubridge and Ball. It read: 'Rear Admiral, Lord Nelson, K.B., Commander of his Britannic Majesty's fleet in the Bay of Naples acquaints the rebellious subjects of his Sicilian Majesty's in the castles of Uovo and Nuovo that he will not permit them to embark or quit those places. They

OPPOSITE Rear-Admiral Sir Thomas Troubridge who told Cardinal Ruffo of Nelson's intention to break the armistice signed with the Jacobins.

must surrender themselves to His Majesty's royal mercy.'

Ruffo, showing that a cardinal can have as acute a sense of honour as an admiral, refused to sign. He had done 'what he thought best for the king's service', having negotiated 'as best he could in his weak state, to save the city of Naples from destruction'. Ruffo was obdurate. 'If Lord Nelson breaks the armistice', Troubridge asked him, 'will your Eminence assist him in his attack with men or with guns?' The answer was an unequivocal negative. That decision was repeated when Ruffo and Nelson met aboard the *Foudroyant* on 25 June. William Hamilton, acting as interpreter, had no doubts where his sympathies lay: 'Lord Nelson is so accustomed to dealings fair and open, that he has no patience when he meets with the contrary, which one must always expect when one has to deal with Italians.'

It may be that for the next three days Nelson agonised about where both duty and honour lay. Certainly there was talk of a compromise which would allow the Jacobins to return to their homes and enable Cardinal Ruffo to attack the French garrison at St Elmo with a clear conscience. But on 28 June all speculation of that sort stopped. Emma Hamilton received a letter from the Neapolitan Queen expressing dismay at the prospect of a compact with the rebels. Nelson was urged 'to treat Naples as if it were a rebellious Irish town'. It was an injunction that appealed to Nelson's temperament and judgment. Jacobins who, believing themselves protected by the truce, had embarked for their evacuation, were captured in their boats. Summary executions immediately began.

Admiral Prince Francesco Caracciolo, one time Commodore of the Neapolitan Navy, was the most celebrated of the victims. Caracciolo had fled from Naples with King Ferdinand, but after a few weeks in Palermo he had gone back to the mainland 'to protect his estates'. Although he promised a swift return to the exiled Court, he remained in Naples long after the French army had left. Eventually he agreed to command a flotilla of gunboats in defence of the Parthenopian Republic against the harassment of the British fleet. When Naples eventually capitulated, he attempted to escape, but was betrayed, captured and brought aboard the *Foudroyant* 'pale, with a long beard, half dead and with downcast eyes'. Captain Hardy had his manacles removed and insisted that he be treated with courtesy. Admiral Nelson convened an immediate court-martial composed entirely of royalist officers.

There were no witnesses, no defence council. Caracciolo's plea that he had no choice other than commanding the gunboats or death was dismissed. He was hanged the same day from the yard-arm of *La Minerve* and his body thrown into the Bay of Naples.

It is impossible to imagine Nelson's retrospective judgment on his own decision to ignore the solemnly negotiated truce and impose the severest penalties on the unprepared Jacobins. His behaviour was certainly condoned and supported by the Admiralty on whose behalf Lord Spencer wrote 'I can only repeat what I believe I have before said on the subject – namely that the intentions and motives by which all your measures have been governed, have been as pure and good, as their success has been complete.' But a year later a mighty voice was raised against him in the House of Commons. Charles James Fox rose during a debate on the Terror in Revolutionary France: 'I wish the atrocities of which we hear so much and which I abhor as much as any man, were indeed unexampled. I fear they do not belong exclusively to the French. When the Right Honourable Gentleman speaks of the extraordinary successes of the last campaign he does not mention the horrors by which some of these successes were accompanied. Naples for instance. . . .'

The French garrison on St Elmo surrendered in early July. On the day of victory, Nelson received a dispatch from Lord Keith, his new Commander-in-Chief, ordering him to proceed at once to Port Mahon. Keith believed Minorca was in danger of invasion. Nelson did not, so he refused to sail, insisting that even if his judgment were wrong, it was 'better to save the Kingdom of Naples, and risk Minorca, than to risk the Kingdom of Naples to save Minorca'. Straightforward disobedience was the sort of conduct Nelson would not tolerate from others but by the turn of the century he had begun to believe that his behaviour need not be governed by the code that circumscribed ordinary men's lives. His commitment to Naples, its Court and its principal courtesan transcended all other loyalties. That irresponsibility he tried to part justify, part deny in his letter of explanation to Lord Keith: 'I am fully aware of the act I have committed, but, sensible of my loyal intentions, I am prepared for any fate which may await my disobedience. . . . Do not think, my dear Lord, that my opinion is formed from the arrangements of any one. No, be it good, or be it bad, it is all my own.'

Nelson's house on the Bronte estate in Sicily. The estate and a Neapolitan dukedom were gifts from King Ferdinand.

Nelson's opinion was often faulty and his judgment of people and events frequently wrong. But his luck was superb. Had the French attacked Minorca, and Nelson had no reason to believe they would not, the island would have fallen, Nelson would have been cashiered. But the attack did not come and Nelson continued sublimely confident that a special providence had made him the one man in the fleet exempted from obedience to the rules of both the service and society.

Inevitably, the relationship between Horatio Nelson and Emma Hamilton was becoming notorious. Emma continued to flatter and pamper the Admiral, presiding at the celebrations to mark the anniversary of the battle of the Nile and urging him to accept the duchy of Bronte that Ferdinand had offered together with its annual dues of £3,000. Nelson was

reluctant to accept a foreign title. The King was insistent. 'Lord Nelson', he asked, 'do you wish that your name alone should pass with honour to posterity; and that I, Ferdinand Bourbon, should appear ungrateful?' Nelson relented and graciously accepted. The discovery that Bronte meant 'thunder' made the title particularly attractive. He began to sign letters 'Bronte Nelson', 'Bronte Nelson of the Nile'. Then, finally and permanently, he became 'Bronte and Nelson'.

Nelson spent the next two months sailing out of Palermo, anxious for King Ferdinand to return to Naples, desperate to serve on another station but fearful of losing Emma Hamilton's company. On shore his behaviour became an increasing embarrassment to his friends. Captain Troubridge was explicit:

> Your Lordship is a stranger to half that happens and the talk it occasions. If you knew what your friends feel for you, I am sure you would cut out all the nocturnal parties. The gambling of the people of Palermo is publicly talked of everywhere. I beseech your Lordship to leave off. I wish my pen could tell you my feelings, I am sure you would oblige me. Lady Hamilton's character will suffer; nothing can prevent people from talking. A gambling woman in the eyes of the English is lost.

At sea he pined for Emma's company. Even the capture of *Le Genereux*, one of the two French ships to escape destruction or capture in Aboukir Bay, was only small consolation. After the victory Captain Ball wrote to the Hamiltons of the 'heaven-born Admiral upon whom fortune smiles wherever he goes'. Nelson himself wrote that 'to say how much I miss your house and company would be saying little – I am not happy anywhere else but with you, nor have I an idea that I ever can be'.

In the late spring, Sir William Hamilton learned that he was to be replaced at the Court of Naples. Nelson had no further interest in remaining at Palermo. His anxiety for recall to home waters was conveyed to Lord Spencer. The First Lord responded almost at once, believing that he was 'joined in my opinion by all your friends here, that you will be more likely to recover your health and strength in England than in an inactive situation at a Foreign Court'. It was a special sort of inactivity that particularly annoyed Lord Keith who had by now become 'bored by Lord Nelson [asking] for permission to take the Queen to Palermo and prince and

princesses to all parts of the globe' and insisted that 'Lady
Hamilton had command of the Fleet long enough.' But some
were sorry to see him go. The crew of the *Foudroyant*'s barge
sent their Admiral a valedictory message:

My Lord, it is with extreme grief that we find you are about to
leave us. We have been along with you (although not in the same
ship) in every Engagement your Lordship has been in, both by
sea and land; and most humbly beg of your Lordship to permit us
to go to England, as your Boat's crew in any ship or vessel, or in
any way that may seem most pleasing to your Lordship. My Lord,
pardon the rude style of Seamen, who are but little acquainted
with writing.

The journey home was made part by land, part by sea.
The Queen of Naples was anxious to visit her scattered relations in European Courts and urge greater efforts against the
French. Lady Hamilton was anxious to accompany her for
part of the journey, displaying her captive hero in the capitals
at which they called. Nelson was willing to be made captive,
displayed and dragged half-way across Europe on his way to
England. Wherever they travelled, people came in their
thousands to see the most famous sailor in the world. The
establishment were scandalised by his willingness to be
exhibited and astonished by his apparent ignorance of the
sensation that the liaison with Emma Hamilton was causing.

At Vienna 'the door of his house was always crowded with
people'. But the British Minister, Lord Minto, recorded 'He
does not seem at all conscious of the sort of discredit he has
fallen into, or the cause of it, for he writes still, not wisely,
about Lady Hamilton and all that. . . . All this is against them
all, but they do not seem conscious.' At Dresden the picture
was much the same. Mrs Melesina St George, a friend of the
British Minister, recorded her impressions of the party:

It is plain that Lord Nelson thinks of nothing but Lady Hamilton, who is totally occupied by the same object. Sir William is old,
infirm, all admiration of his wife, and never spoke but to applaud
her. . . . After dinner we had several songs in honour of Lord
Nelson, written by Miss Knight and sung by Lady Hamilton. She
puffs the incense full in his face; but he receives it with pleasure
and snuffs it up very cordially.

Nelson landed in Yarmouth on 6 November and received a
welcome no less rapturous than those he had enjoyed all the
way across Europe. The horses were removed from the shafts
of his carriage at the dock gates, and members of the rejoicing

crowd drew it to *The Wrestlers Arms* which the landlord asked permission to rename *The Nelson Arms*. 'That would be absurd', the honoured guest replied, 'seeing that I have but one' and sat down to write two immediate letters. The Admiralty were told of his desire to serve at sea again: 'I trust that my necessary journey, by land, from the Mediterranean, will not be considered as a wish to be a moment out of active service.' His wife was assured of his continuing affection: 'We are this moment arrived and the post only allows me to say that we shall set off tomorrow noon, and be with you on Saturday, to dinner. I have only had time to open one of your letters, my visits are so numerous.'

The effect Lord Nelson's letter had on his wife is uncertain. Lord St Vincent recorded his opinion on the letter the Admiralty received in a note to the Board's Secretary:

It is evident from Lord Nelson's letter to you on his landing that he is doubtful of the propriety of his conduct. I have no doubt he is pledged to getting Lady Hamilton received at St James's, and everywhere, and that he will get into much brouillerie about it. Troubridge says Lord Spencer talks of putting him in a two-decked ship. If he does, he cannot give him a separate command, for he cannot bear confinement to any object; he is a partisan; his ship is always in the most dreadful disorder, and never can become an officer fit to be placed where I am. . . .

Bad as his professional position had become, personal matters were in even greater disarray. Nelson and his entourage arrived in London on 9 November – having mistakenly first made for Norfolk in the belief that the reunion was to be there. At Nerot's Hotel, in King Street, St James's, Lady Nelson met Lady Hamilton for the first time. Emma immediately felt 'an antipathy not to be described' and Nelson began a time so desperate that he later confessed that 'Sooner than live the unhappy life I did when I last came to England, I would stay abroad for ever.'

The Nelsons and the Hamiltons met each day. Emma seemed unmoved by the refusal of London society to admit her. When Sir William Hamilton went to Court he went alone, as the royal family would not receive his wife. King George made his disapproval of Nelson public. At his first soirée, the King made a short inquiry about Nelson's health and turned away to join a junior officer in rapt discussion. After half an hour, Collingwood wondered which of the officer's qualities had so excited the King's interest, as their

LEFT Sir William Hamilton; studio of Reynolds.

RIGHT The family of Ferdinand IV, King of Naples, by Angelica Kauffmann.

RIGHT The British fleet at anchor in the Bay of Naples, by Guardi. Nelson's obsessive preoccupation with the Neapolitan Court and the English camp-followers became notorious. In 1801 Lord Keith decided 'Lady Hamilton has commanded the fleet long enough.'

conversation 'could not have been about his success'. Nelson admitted to Emma, 'I found St James's as cold as the atmosphere.'

Naturally, but unreasonably, as the embarrassment turned to despair, much of the blame for Nelson's unhappy condition was heaped on his wife. Lady Spencer could remember the days when Horatio and Fanny asked to sit next to each other at dinner. Lord Nelson had become detached towards his wife to the point at which his conduct was offensive. 'Such a contrast, I never saw', Lady Spencer wrote. When Fanny fainted at the theatre, her father-in-law took her home while her husband remained with the Hamiltons to watch the rest of the play. Lord Nelson spent Christmas with the Hamiltons. The invitation, delivered by Emma, did not include Fanny. Lady Nelson passed the festive season alone. Her husband, by any standards, exhibited a callous disregard for the welfare and happiness of his wife. But despite his wanton lack of feeling, he did not completely escape the trauma that comes from divided loyalties and conflicting obligations. One night, 'in a state of absolute despair and distraction [he] rambled as far as the city; perambulated Fleet Market, Blackfriars Bridge etc, and exhausted with fatigue, as well as overpowered by mental suffering, reached the House of Sir William Hamilton in Grosvenor Square about four in the morning'.

A total and final break with Fanny had to come. Almost half a century after it took place, William Haselwood, an attorney who claimed to have been present, by chance, at the final agonising moment, recorded his version of how the parting came. It does less than justice to the abandoned wife who had suffered neglect and humiliation beyond endurance.

A cheerful conversation was passing on indifferent subjects when Lord Nelson spoke of something which had been done or said by 'dear Lady Hamilton'. Lady Nelson rose from her chair and exclaimed with much vehemence, 'I am sick of hearing of dear Lady Hamilton, and am resolved that you shall give up either her or me.' Lord Nelson, with perfect calmness, said: 'Take care, Fanny, what you say. I love you sincerely; but I cannot forget my obligations to Lady Hamilton, or speak of her otherwise than with affection and admiration.' Without saying one soothing word, but muttering something about her mind being made up, Lady Nelson left the room, and shortly after drove from the house. They never lived together again. I believe Lord Nelson took a formal leave of her Ladyship before joining the Fleet under Sir Hyde

Parker; but that to the day of her husband's death, she never made any apology for her abrupt and ungentle conduct above related, or any overture towards a reconciliation.

Nelson needed to be back at sea, to escape the pressure of London and to seek emotional rest and regeneration. Fortunately, despite his low standing with the Board of Admiralty, the opportunity came. Nelson's fighting record was second to none. England was still at war with France. He was still needed in the Mediterranean. In January 1801 *The London Gazette* announced that he was to return to those waters as second-in-command to Admiral Sir Hyde Parker and had been promoted to Vice-Admiral of the Blue.

5
The Honour of England
1801

ADMIRAL SIR HORATIO NELSON and his Reverend brother William set out for Southampton on 13 January 1801. Horatio was never to see his wife again, but the formalities of marital obligation were still observed. The customary letter was written and dispatched as soon as the brothers had established themselves in their lodgings: 'My dear Fanny, We are arrived and heartily tired; and with kindest regards to my father and all the family believe me, your affectionate, Nelson.'

The next day both brothers were in Plymouth. Admiral Nelson found St Vincent in high spirits and they proved infectious. Nelson's ship, the *San Josef* was reported ready for sea although, Captain Hardy told him, the Admiral's cabin was not yet fitted out. Although the crew believed they were proceeding with all speed, Nelson declared himself dissatisfied with the work rate. The *San Josef* must be anchored alongside the Commander-in-Chief's flagship in Torbay harbour within seven days. It tied up alongside St Vincent on 1 February and received his orders. He was to transfer to a smaller ship, the *St George*, and become Sir Hyde Parker's second-in-command on an expedition to the Baltic. There was deep disappointment at again being given second place and only slight comfort from the promise that on his return, the *San Josef* would be his again.

The Baltic expedition was Britain's reaction to the renewed hostility from the reformed and resuscitated League of Armed Neutrality. In 1780, Russia, Prussia, Denmark and Sweden had formed the League as a reaction to Britain's aggressive maritime policy. It had never been able to match the power of the British Navy acting in support of British trade and had gradually become moribund. From 1798 to 1800 Britain simply refused to recognise non-belligerent status. Neutral ships carrying cargo to France or French prizes were seized. By 1800 neutral patience was running out. Napoleon exploited their frustration and urged them to take positive action in their own defence. During the dying days of the century, Britain's right to search and seize neutral ships was formally challenged. If the challenge went unanswered, Britannia's right to rule the waves would be in doubt.

The League announced the new rules under which its members would operate. Neutrals would be free to trade with whomever they chose. Neutral ships would never be searched and their cargoes would not be seized. Britain would no longer be allowed to treat naval stores as contraband. The League claimed a hundred ships of the line to reinforce their words with deeds. If necessary, France would be blockaded. In any event, the Baltic was to be closed to British merchantmen. To prove that he really meant business, the Tsar impounded all British merchantmen in Russia and confiscated their cargoes. Pitt asked the House of Commons if 'we are to suffer neutral nations, by hoisting a flag upon a sloop or fishing boat to convey the treasures of South America to the harbours of Spain or the naval stores of the Pacific to Brest or Toulon'. But on 1 February 1801, Nelson was asking himself more personal questions. He had to decide what must be done in the light of Emma Hamilton's letter announcing the birth of a child they had conceived aboard the *Foudroyant* the previous April: the single survivor of twins.

It was a girl. Immediately after her birth she was christened Horatia, the only visible sign of her parentage that was ever openly given. A complicated subterfuge was arranged to enable coded messages about the girl's progress to be passed from mother to father. A sailor called Thompson (and occasionally Thomson) was invented who was said to be the father of an illegitimate child, the product of a lasting union that could not be solemnised because the lady's rich uncle forbade marriage. "Thompson" sailed with Nelson, and Emma looked after his baby. Being compassionate, she relayed messages about the health and welfare of both mother and baby through the Admiral.

There can be no certainty how many people the unlikely story deceived. It seems inconceivable that the ageing William Hamilton believed the story to be anything but a lie. But even if he knew of his wife's pregnancy, which is by no means certain, many of her closest friends did not. Lady Hamilton had two advantages during her months of conscious deception. She had a figure described by Lord Minto as 'monstrous for its enormity'. She was also a superlative and practised liar.

Horatia was not, as she had convinced Nelson, Lady Hamilton's first or only child. The product of a previous liaison, Emma Carew, was almost adult. She lived in the north of England totally unaware, as her mother probably was, of her father's name. About that, Nelson never found out. All of Emma's secrets would have remained part of her hidden life had she kept her word to Nelson and burned his letters.

Shortly before his daughter's birth, Nelson had written to her mother, 'I burn all your dear letters. It is right for your sake and I wish that you would burn all mine. They can do no good and will do us both harm, for any seizure of them, or the dropping of even one of them would fill the mouths of the world sooner than we intended.' It was advice that, despite his pretensions to honour, Nelson thought right to give. For his character enabled him to believe that honour was a substance which he could shape and mould to his own convenience. Emma's character made her reaction certain. She was too foolish to accept the advice and pathologically incapable of not pretending that she had.

Because of her irresponsible inconstancy, we are able to read Nelson's reaction to the birth of his daughter:

I believe poor dear Mrs Thompson's friend will go mad with joy. He cries, prays and performs all tricks, yet does not show any of his feelings. . . . He swears he will drink your health this day in a bumper and damn me if I don't join him despite all the doctors in Europe . . . I cannot write, I am so delighted by this young man at my elbow. I believe he is foolish, he does nothing but rave about you and her.

During the next few days there were repeated offers of marriage 'as soon as possible'. Three weeks later he insisted that 'If you was single and I found you under a hedge, I would instantly marry you.' Without doubt that, at least, was true. Nelson remained infatuated, convinced, like any schoolboy, that every man in the world was in hot pursuit of his sweetheart. For months he had been obsessed with fear that the Prince Regent would seduce her. On 20 January, less than a week before the birth of Horatia, he had written Emma a letter full of agitation and double standards:

I own I wonder that Sir William should have a wish for the Prince of Wales to come under your roof, no good can come from it but every harm. You are too beautiful not to have enemies, and even one visit will stamp you as his 'chere amie', and we know he is dotingly fond of such women as yourself, and is without one spark of honour in those respects and would leave you to bewail your folly. . . . But my dear friend, I know you too well not to be convinced you cannot be seduced by any Prince in Europe. You are, in my opinion, the pattern of perfection.

That perfection was not unblemished by jealousy. As if in response to Nelson's possessiveness, Emma began to insist that he never dined ashore if there were to be women present

OPPOSITE Horatia Nelson – conceived aboard the *Foudroyant* during April 1801; a complicated subterfuge was arranged to explain her presence in the Hamilton household.

Ah where & ah where is my gallant Sailor gone?. }DIDO in Despair{ He's gone to figh the Frenchmen & loose t'other Arm & L
He's gone to Fight the Frenchmen for George upon y Throne. And left me here with old Antique to lay me down &

Emma Hamilton – with a figure 'monstrous for its enormity' – was popularly recognised as Nelson's mistress despite all her protestations of innocence and chastity.

at the dinner. He agreed that he would dine in mixed company only with Emma's consent. Such precautions were, he assured Lady Hamilton, unnecessary. 'With my present feelings I might be trusted with fifty virgins naked in a dark room.'

On 23 February with the fleet almost ready to sail north, Nelson dashed to London to see Emma and Horatia. He arrived at 23 Piccadilly at 7 a.m. the following morning, 'almost beside himself with expectation'. Emma was unwell, the victim of her characteristic insistence on living an active life too soon after a difficult birth. The child was in the care of a Mrs Gibson. Nelson's Dover Street house being locked and shuttered, he hurried three times each day between Latham's

Hotel in Albemarle Street, the Hamiltons' house in Piccadilly and the home of Mrs Gibson at 9 Great Tichfield Street, where he doted on his daughter, insisting that 'A finer child never was produced by any two persons. It was in truth a love begotten child.' He was careful for her future welfare, arranging for the William Nelsons to stay near by, even though it was necessary to warn Emma that the 'Reverend Sir you will find a great bore at times.' And discretion was not abandoned. It was important, Lady Hamilton was reminded, that nobody should believe 'that Sir William maintains the family of the Nelsons which would vex me'.

On 26 February Nelson received orders to return to the *St George*, take on board six hundred troops and sail for Yarmouth, there to join Sir Hyde Parker. He left at once and, assuring Emma that he had 'no fear of death, except of parting from you', drove through the night to Spithead. On the day the *St George* weighed anchor, he wrote to Lady Hamilton:

Now my own dear wife, for such you are in my eyes and in the face of heaven, I can give full scope to my feelings. . . . You know my dearest Emma that there is nothing in this world that I would not do for us to live together and have our dear child with us. I firmly believe that this campaign will give us peace, and then we will set off for Bronte. . . . We must manage till we can quit this country or your 'uncle' dies. I love, I never did love anyone else. I never had a dear pledge of love till you gave me one, and you thank God, never gave one to anyone else. . . . You, my dearest Emma and my Country are the dearest objects of my heart – a heart susceptible and true. . . . My longing for you, both person and conversation you may readily imagine. What must be my sensation at the thought of sleeping with you! it sets me on fire, even the thoughts much more would the reality. I am sure my love and desires are all to you, and if any woman naked were to come to me, even as I am this moment from thinking of you, I hope it might rot off if I would touch her even with my hand. No, my heart, person and mind is in perfect union of love towards my own, dear beloved Emma.

And so it was, as Lady Nelson realised when she received a letter written three days after the *St George* had put to sea:

I have done my duty as an honest generous man, and I neither want nor wish for anybody to care what becomes of me, whether I return, or am left in the Baltic. Living, I have done all in my power for you, and if dead, you will find that I have done the same; therefore my only wish is to be left to myself; and wishing you every happiness, believe that I am your affectionate Nelson and Bronte.

Fanny read it and wrote a note at the foot of the last page.
'This is my Lord Nelson's letter of dismissal.'

Within minutes of his arrival in Portsmouth, Nelson had
announced his intention of setting sail for Yarmouth on the
first tide. The 49th Regiment of Foot and a company of
riflemen were embarked and their commanding officer,
Lt-Colonel the Hon. William Stewart, began to write his
detailed account of the Copenhagen campaign and the
behaviour of the Admiral whose efforts crowned it with
victory:

> His Lordship [Stewart noted] was rather too apt to interfere in
> the workings of the Ship and not always with the best success or
> judgement. The wind, when off Dungeness, was scanty, and the
> Ship was to be put about; Lord Nelson *would* give the order and
> caused her to miss stays. Upon this he said rather peevishly to the
> Master or Officer of the Watch: 'Well, now, see what we have done.
> Well Sir, what do you mean to do?' The Officer saying with hesita-
> tion: 'I don't exactly know my lord; I fear she won't do', Lord
> Nelson turned sharply towards the cabin and replied: 'Well, I am
> sure if you don't know what to do with her, no more do I either.'
> He then went in, leaving the Officer to work the ship as he liked.

The *St George* arrived in the Yarmouth Roads on 6 March.
The fleet was all activity, but the preparations which en-
grossed the Commander-in-Chief did not concern the Armed
Neutrality of the North. There was a new young Lady Hyde
Parker and the Admiral was both loath to leave her and
determined to depart in style. A farewell ball had been
arranged for 13 March.

It had never been Nelson's practice to react to the orders of
his superiors with the unthinking obedience he expected in
others. Loyalty was reserved for those who, in Nelson's
judgment, deserved it. Hyde Parker did not. So a letter was
dispatched to Troubridge, by then a member of the Board of
Admiralty:

> If a Lord of the Admiralty – and such a Lord – had not told me
> that the Baltic fleet had order to put to sea, I would not have
> believed it, and forgive me, I even think seriously that, by some
> accident, they have not arrived, for there is not the least appear-
> ance of going. . . . I know, my dear Troubridge, how angry the
> Earl [St Vincent] would be if he knew I, as second-in-command,
> was to venture to give an opinion for I know his opinion of officers
> writing to the Admiralty. But what I say is in the mouth of the old
> market women at Yarmouth. . . . Consider how nice it must be

laying in bed with a young wife, compared to a damned cold raw wind.

What the old market women would have said had its desired effect. Earl St Vincent had no intention of allowing Hyde Parker 'to eat his "batter pudding" as the fair Fanny is called' and ordered him to sea, 'an hour after the wind would permit sailing'. Nelson was delighted and wrote in jubilation to Troubridge: 'Now we can have no desire for staying for her Ladyship is gone, and the ball for Friday night is knocked by you and the earl's impoliteness to send gentlemen to sea instead of dancing in nice white gloves.' The fleet sailed for the Baltic on 12 March with the Commander-in-Chief who was reluctant to go and a second-in-command who had no confidence in his commanding officer. The day after the fleet set sail, Nelson began what was to be a continual correspondence of complaint: 'The fleet in general keeps very badly their station, for although the Commander-in-Chief made the signal for close order of sailing, yet scarcely one have kept their stations and in particular the good going ships.' Three days later, a letter noted the sort of situation which always excited Nelson to what he believed to be righteous anger: 'I have not yet seen my Commander-in-Chief and have had no official communication whatsoever. All I have gathered of our first plans I disapprove most exceedingly; honour may arise from them, good cannot.'

Although Nelson did not know it, Hyde Parker possessed specific instructions. The Danes must be made to agree to British demands either by 'amicable arrangements or by actual hostilities'. Then, the Danes being overcome by negotiation or force of arms, he was to sail on and attack the Russians. These orders Hyde Parker took to mean that his first duty was to attempt a negotiated peace. As he sailed north that, unknown to Nelson, was his primary intention.

On 18 March, the fleet (battered by storms and with its sailors suffering from the sudden transition from Mediterranean to Baltic weather) reached the Naze. During the next day, the ships formed up at the Skaw where the Kattegat stretches south to Zealand, and Nicholas Vansittart sailed ahead in the *London* to tell the Danes that although a diplomatic solution was Britain's wish, if it could not be obtained within forty-eight hours, battle was the certain outcome.

Even that ultimatum did not satisfy Nelson, who admitted to Vansittart that he 'hated your pen and ink men' and

Admiral Sir Hyde Parker by George Romney – 'I will make a signal to withdraw for Nelson's sake. If he is in a condition to continue the action successfully he will disregard it.'

believed that the fleet should be influencing the outcome of the diplomacy. The negotiators might be allowed to sit briefly around their table but 'The Dane should see our Flag waving every moment he lifted up his head.' In any event, Nelson had simple views on all such negotiations: 'A fleet of British men-of-war are the best negotiations in Europe.'

On 20 March the fleet was ready for battle, and a favourable wind would have driven it swiftly between the Danish and Swedish shore batteries, but Hyde Parker waited for news of Vansittart's mission. By the morning of 22 March, Vansittart having still not returned with news of the negotiations, the fleet sailed a mile farther north and anchored again off Nekke Head. The next day the *London* was sighted making slow progress against the wind. When it rejoined the fleet, Vansittart reported that negotiations had failed. The Northern Confederation would not willingly be dissolved.

A council of war was called aboard the *London*. Before he rowed across to join his Commander-in-Chief, Nelson wrote home to Emma: 'Now we are sure of fighting, I am sent for.

When it was a joke, I was kept in the background: tomorrow will, I hope, be a proud day for England.' Nelson climbed aboard the *London*, certain of the advice he would give and contemptuous of a Commander-in-Chief who needed to ask about the best course of action for 'If a man consults whether he is to fight, when he has the power in his own hands, *it is certain that his opinion is against fighting.*'

Most members of the Council of War were deeply despondent. Lieutenant Laymen later noted in his diary that 'All heads were very gloomy.' Vansittart had reported more than diplomatic failure. He had seen strong fortifications all around Copenhagen and observed heavy batteries on Elsinore Point. The Danish fleet was, he believed, strongest at its head. Nelson had met such difficulties before. At Aboukir Bay, where there had been heavy batteries and an enemy most powerful in the van, the batteries had been run and the attack directed at the rear. Certainly Nelson initially considered, and perhaps even advocated, such a tactic. But a surprise attack at the rear could be carried out successfully only by entering the Baltic through the Great Belt. That involved too great a loss of time. Nelson became convinced that at all costs the battle must begin before the Danes strengthened their defences.

The plan he eventually advocated involved the detachment of a squadron from the fleet to sail up the Baltic to engage and hold the Russians at Reval while the rest of the fleet challenged the Danes at Copenhagen. Nelson tried to insist at least on swift action, being 'of the opinion [that] the boldest measures are the safest; and that our country demands a most vigorous exertion of her force, directed with judgment'. But judgment seemed less important than vigour. His final comment on the Council of War was part acquiescence, part defiance: 'I don't care a damn by which passage we go so long as we fight them.'

But the tactical argument was not quite over. Back on board the *St George*, Nelson composed a memorandum to Hyde Parker:

My dear Sir Hyde,

The conversation we had yesterday has naturally, from its importance, been the subject of my thoughts; and the more I have reflected, the more I am confirmed in opinion that not a moment should be lost in attacking the Enemy. . . .

There followed a number of closely and lucidly argued alternative battle plans, from which Hyde Parker was invited to choose in the certainty that whatever decision was made, at least in battle he could be sure of his second-in-command's loyalty: 'In supporting you, my dear Sir Hyde, through the arduous and important task you have undertaken, no exertion of head or heart shall be wanting from your most obedient and faithful servant, Nelson and Bronte.'

Hyde Parker remained unwilling to adopt Nelson's boldest strategy. But five days later the Nelson tactic for attack on Copenhagen was accepted. Nelson reacted with a typical absence of humility. He explained his reaction in a letter to Emma: 'Sir Hyde Parker has by this time found out the worth of your Nelson and that he is a useful sort of man on a pinch: therefore, if he has ever thought unkindly of me, I freely forgive him. Nelson must stand among the first or he must fall.'

On the evening of 26 March 1801 the British fleet anchored six miles above Cronenburg. Vice-Admiral Nelson was given command of ten sail of the line, four frigates, four sloops, seven 'bombs', two fire-ships and twelve gun-brigs to be employed in a tactical assault on Copenhagen. Nelson moved his flag from the *St George* to the *Elephant* whose Captain, Thomas Foley, had served under him at the battle of the Nile. For three days, although ready for battle, the British fleet lay becalmed off the Sound, and the Danes strengthened their fortifications.

At daybreak on 30 March the wind changed and a breeze from the north-west carried the fleet down the Channel in single file. Nelson's division was in the van. Hyde Parker had the middle station. Admiral Graves commanded the rear. The batteries on the Danish shore opened fire immediately the *Monarch*, the leading British ship, was within range. The Swedish guns, however, remained silent, so the fleet swung hard against the west coast and out of range of the Elsinore batteries. Nelson wrote to Emma that 'More powder and shot, I believe, never was thrown away for not one single shot struck a ship of the British fleet. Some of our ships fired: but the *Elephant* did not return a single shot. I hope to reserve them for a better occasion.'

About that better occasion, Nelson was confident. The Danish defences looked 'formidable to those who are children at war, but to my judgement with ten sail-of-the-line, I think I can annihilate them; at all events, I hope to be allowed to try'.

132

Nelson's judgment about the dangers of delay was proved
right. Colonel Stewart, in command of the infantry Nelson
had taken aboard in England, 'perceived that our delay had
been of important advantage to the enemy, who had lined the
Northern edge of the shoals near the Crown batteries and the
front of the harbour and arsenal, with a formidable flotilla'.
Seaward of the harbour mouth was an unbroken line of un-
masted warships and floating batteries. On their northern
flank they were supported by the battery at Trekröner and a
small squadron of warships. A bombardment of the city
could not begin before these defences were broken.

In fact, the British hoped to avoid a major bombardment of

133

Copenhagen. Hyde Parker was rightly more concerned with destroying the Danish power to interfere with British commerce than with razing Denmark's capital to the ground. As bombardment was not his first choice, once bombardment became dangerous and difficult he considered other possibilities. At a second Council of War on 31 March, Nelson's plan was accepted. The ten lightest ships of the line and all the frigates would sail eastwards and having established position in the Middle Ground would approach the city through the shallow and narrow King's Deep.

The strategy was an adaptation of the plan which had worked so well at the Nile. The enemy would face attack from a wholly unexpected direction mounted against the weakest point of an over-extended line. If all went according to plan, the wind which carried Nelson through the King's Deep would bear him back to reunion with Admiral Hyde Parker.

The nights of 30 and 31 March were spent in secret sounding and buoying of the channels around the Middle Ground. Nelson himself worked assiduously to make sure that the preparations were complete. The surgeon on board the *Elephant*, 'during the interval that preceded the Battle . . . could only silently admire . . . the first man in all the world spending hours of the day and night in the Boats amid floating ice; and in the severest weather: and wonder when the light showed me a path marked by buoys which had been trackless the preceding evening'.

On 1 April the whole British fleet stood prepared for battle at the north-eastern limit of the Middle Ground. At 1 p.m. Nelson gave the signal to weigh anchor and the *Amazon* led the fleet through the Hollander Deep. By nightfall the whole fleet was in position two miles from the head of the Danish line. It was a moment for bravura and a time for careful planning. So, having announced 'I will fight them the moment I have a fair wind', Nelson began to draw up his precise plan of battle.

The three leading British men-of-war, the *Edgar*, *Agamemnon* and *Isis*, were to open fire on the three southernmost Danes as they sailed past them and then anchor opposite the fifth, sixth and seventh ships in the enemy line. The *Ardent* and the *Glatton*, the fourth and fifth British ships, were then to concentrate their fire on the first four Danish vessels and continue to fire into them until they were beaten out of the line. As each section of the British fleet leapfrogged another, parts of the Danish line would be subject to continuous heavy bombardment and the battle formation would be smashed.

The plan worked less well in practice than in theory. Things started well. A later sailor believed it characteristic of the fortunes of the 'heaven-born admiral, that the wind which had been fair the day before to take him south, changed by the hour of the battle to fair to take him north', but heaven's providence deserted him as soon as the British column set sail. The *Agamemnon* stuck on the Middle Ground. By the time the *Polyphemus* had taken her place, the *Bellona* and the *Russell* had run aground on the starboard shoal. Nelson began the battle with a quarter of his heavy ships out of action.

The Danes fought harder than Nelson had anticipated. The 'weaker' ships at the southern end of their line put up a stiff resistance and the enemy gunnery was of a much higher quality than the British sailors believed possible from any other fleet. Even Nelson admitted it was 'warm work' and told Colonel Stewart that 'This day may be the last to us at any moment. But mark you!' he added 'I would not be elsewhere for thousands!' It got warmer as the British bombardment (with its penetration reduced by the necessity to anchor not in the ideal firing position but at a point free of the shoals) proved less and less effective and the Danes fought on with crews reinforced from the mainland.

By noon things were looking black for the British. The *Monarch* and the *Defiance* were 'dreadfully cut up as they were exposed to the Crown batteries' and under continuous fire from the *Holstein* and *Zealand*, both of which fought on despite heavy losses. That evening Nelson was to confess that 'I have been in a hundred and five engagements, but that of today is the most terrible of them all.'

Hyde Parker, unable to move up and offer Nelson assistance, began to fear that all was lost. If not the most courageous or determined of admirals, he proved, at least according to Southey's biography, the most sensitive and sympathetic of all Nelson's commanders. At one o'clock, he told his Fleet Captain, Domett, 'I will make a signal to recall for Nelson's sake. If he is in a condition to continue the action successfully he will disregard it: if he is not it will be an excuse for his retreat and no blame can be imputed to him.'

In fact the signal to disengage was made just at the moment when the battle was turning Britain's way, but inevitably some sections of the fleet accepted it as their automatic

The Battle of Copenhagen

Nelson considered the battle of Copenhagen his hardest won victory. As second-in-command to Sir Hyde Parker, Nelson attacked the Danish fleet at anchor off Copenhagen while Parker watched from a safe distance. Both sides fought to a standstill with great valour, when Nelson demanded a truce to avoid further casualties.

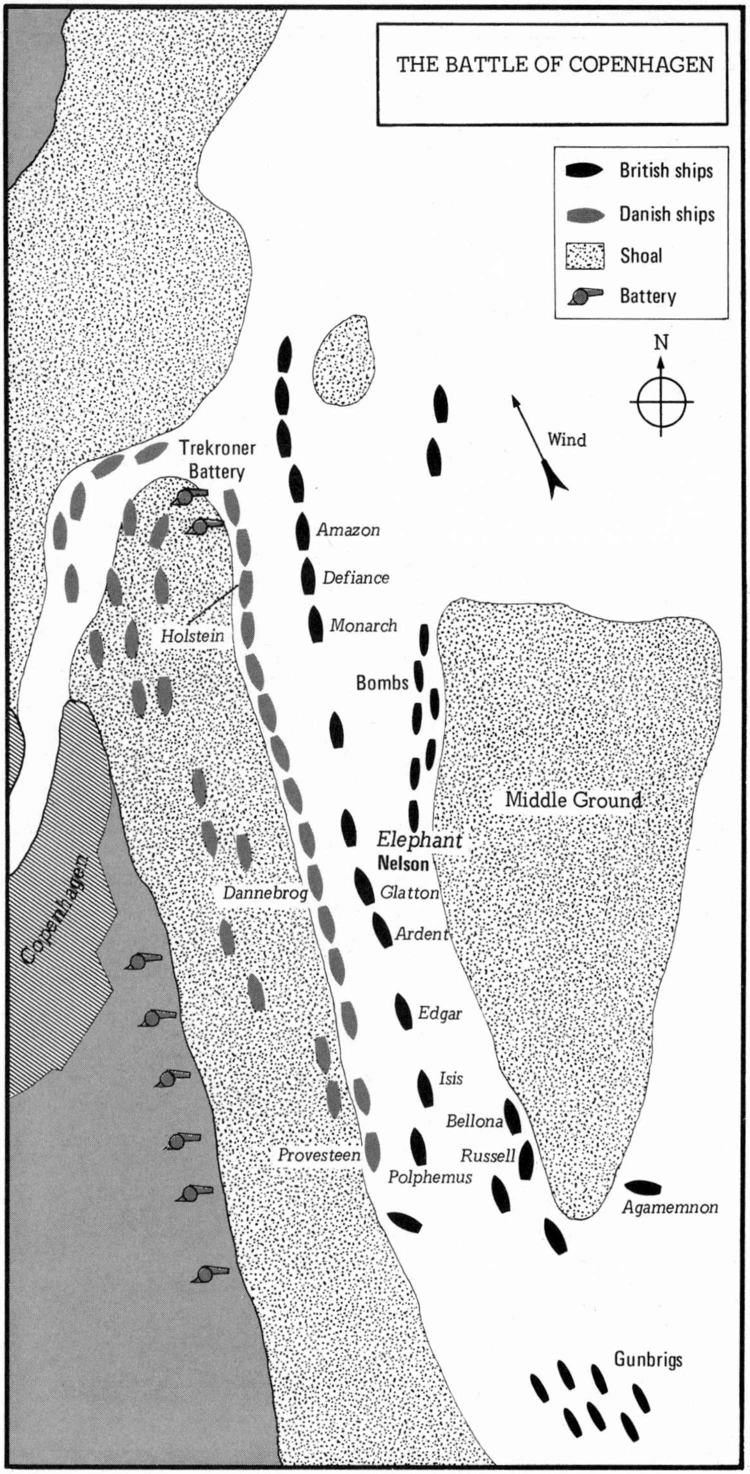

THE BATTLE OF COPENHAGEN

British ships
Danish ships
Shoal
Battery

N

Wind

Trekroner Battery

Amazon

Defiance

Monarch

Holstein

Bombs

Middle Ground

Elephant
Nelson
Glatton

Ardent

Dannebrog

Edgar

Isis

Bellona

Russell

Provesteen

Polphemus

Agamemnon

Copenhagen

Gunbrigs

OPPOSITE ABOVE
The British fleet off Elsinore during their passage through the Sound, by Nicholas Pocock – 'More powder and shot, I believe never was thrown away for not one single shot struck a ship of the British fleet.'

OPPOSITE BELOW
An engraving of the principal Danish officers who served at the battle of Copenhagen.

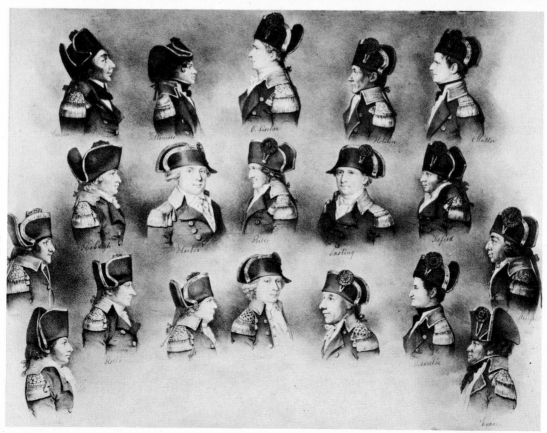

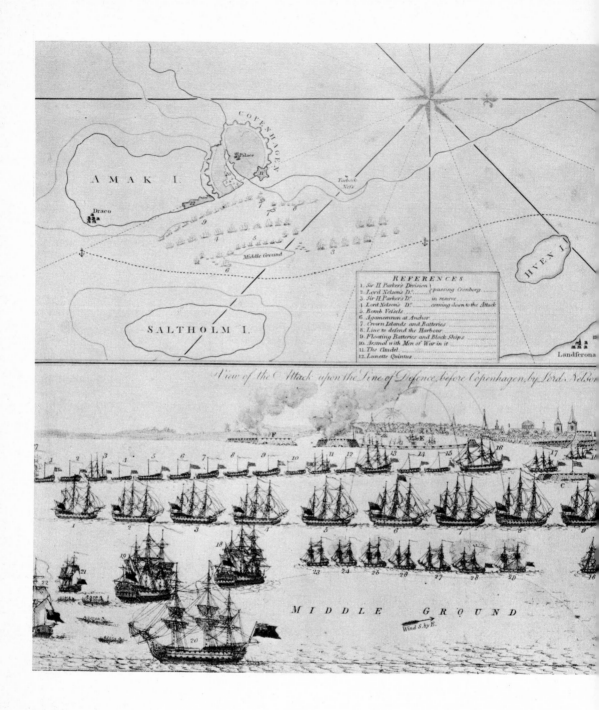

REFERENCES

1. Sir H. Parker's Division \
2. Lord Nelson's D.° *passing Cronborg* \
3. Sir H. Parker's D.° ...... *in reserve* \
4. Lord Nelson's D.° ...... *coming down to the Attack* \
5. Bomb Vessels \
6. Agamemnon at Anchor \
7. Crown Islands and Batteries \
8. Line to defend the Harbour \
9. Floating Batteries and Block Ships \
10. Arsenal with Men of War in it \
11. The Citadel \
12. Lunette Quintus

View of the Attack upon the Line of Defence before Copenhagen, by Lord Nelson

Hyde Parker's fleet in line
of battle. The tactical
dispositions made, the
approach to the Copenhagen
Sound begins.

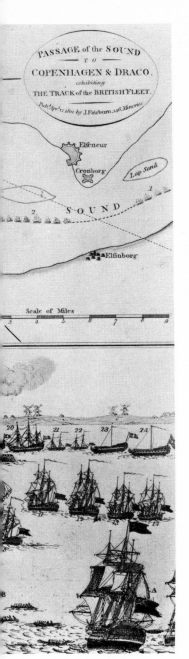

obligation. Captain Riou repeated it to his squadron of frigates seconds before he was killed by fire from the Trekröner batteries. Rear-Admiral Graves repeated the signal to his section, but kept the 'close action' signal flying by its side, for he had noticed that Admiral Nelson in the *Elephant* was not repeating the Commander-in-Chief's order.

The *Elephant* was in simultaneous close combat with the Danish flagship *Dannebrog* and two floating batteries when Signal 39, the order to disengage, was sighted. Stewart asked Nelson if it should be repeated to the fleet. Nelson ordered that it should only be acknowledged and a moment later asked for assurance that Signal 16, 'close action', was still flying. With obvious signs of agitation, he began to mutter half to himself the rhetorical questions 'Do you know what's shown on board the Commander-in-Chief, No. 39? . . . to leave off action . . . Leave off action. Now damn me if I do!' He then turned to Captain Foley. 'You know, Foley, I have only one eye. I have a right to be blind sometimes.' He then put his telescope to his blind eye, 'I really do not see the signal.'

An hour later, most of the Danish fleet were silent. The *Dannebrog* floated in flames, out of control and 'spreading terror through the enemy's lines'. When it blew up at 3.30, Fischer, the Danish Commander-in-Chief, noted that a 'quarter of the line from the Trekröner to the *Hyaelperen* was in the power of the enemy'. It was a victory for tenacity, for the willingness to go on fighting when the fight seemed finished and lost.

The victory was neither glorious nor overwhelming. At the end of the first day, when the cease-fire began and Nelson attempted to slip some of his badly damaged ships past the Trekröner batteries, the *Defiance*, the *Elephant*, the *Desirée* and the *Monarch* all ran aground. At the batteries end, Nelson felt none of the joy in victory that had marked the end of earlier engagements. It was not simply that the victory was inconclusive. Nelson had a special feeling about the French. At Copenhagen, fighting the Danes, he felt none 'of that indignation against the enemy, and that impression of retributive justice which at the Nile had given a sterner temper to his mind'.

The dispatch in which Admiral Graves reported the engagement to the Admiralty put the battle in proper perspective: 'Considering the disadvantages of navigation, the

Captain Riou by J. Jackson; in command of the British frigates at Copenhagen.

approach to the enemy, their vast number of guns and mortars on both land and sea, I do not think there ever was a bolder attack.' There had rarely been a more bloody one. The British fleet lost a thousand men killed and wounded. Estimates of the Danish casualties varied from two to six thousand. Captain Fremantle recorded that 'The carnage aboard the Danish vessels taken exceeds anything I ever heard of, the result of their willingness to stand and fight. Their courage was beyond either doubt or praise.' Nelson paid them his highest tribute: 'The French fought bravely, but they could not have stood for one hour the fight which the Danes supported for four.'

At the end of the four hours of fighting, an uneasy truce was concluded. The Danes, fearing a bombardment of their capital, renewed it each day until the news of the death of the Tsar reached Copenhagen. Then, their loyalty to an old ally was overcome by their wish for permanent peace. A permanent armistice was signed, the Danish Government solemnly promised to refit none of its warships for fourteen weeks and offered the provision of victuals.

Twenty-four hours after the last shot was fired at Copenhagen, Nelson began to agitate for permission to sail on towards the Russian fleet at Reval. While the truce lasted only from day to day, departure was impossible. On 18 April the Treaty was ratified and Nelson felt free to move on but, to his intense exasperation Hyde Parker was not prepared to sail. After an inconclusive action against a Swedish squadron anchored at Kioge Bay, the Commander-in-Chief ordered his fleet to anchor four hundred miles from the Russian fleet.

It was the last order Hyde Parker was to give. On 5 May orders arrived relieving him of his command and appointing Nelson his successor. Forty-eight hours later, the British fleet left Kioge Bay. Next day most of his ships were left at Bornholm Island to prevent the Swedish fleet from sailing north to join the Russians. Ten seventy-four gunners sailed on, under Nelson's own command, for Reval and the Russian fleet. They arrived too late. The ice had melted and the twelve Russian ships the British hoped to destroy had left for Kronstadt.

Nelson's determination to find and sink the Russian fleet had not been rewarded. But his insistence that the Armed Neutrality of the North was wholly dependent on Russian leadership (and would break up without it) was vindicated. Naval defeat might have killed the Russian wish for domination of a northern alliance. The death of the Tsar destroyed it swiftly, and certainly. Alexander I was anxious, not simply to modify, but to reverse completely his father's policies. On 26 March, Admiral Sir Horatio Nelson in command of the British fleet off Rostock received a placatory message from the new Tsar. The war against the Armed Neutrality of the North was over. Nelson, once more in bad health, resigned, struck his flag and sailed for England.

6
'They cannot come by Sea' 1801-5

ADMIRAL NELSON LANDED AT YARMOUTH on 1 July 1801 after a tedious journey made slightly more tolerable by the memory of the toast the fleet had drunk before his departure – 'Let he who is no longer our Commander be our Example.' He was in ill health and low spirits. The first was improved by a short stay in Yarmouth Naval Hospital, the second by a brief fishing holiday with the Hamiltons.

Before the end of the month he was back in naval employment. The treaty of Lunéville between Austria and France had ended the land war in Europe, at least for the moment. But France and Britain had still to negotiate a lasting peace. The prospect of that happening, on terms acceptable to France, seemed (at least to Bonaparte) more likely to come about if the French army at Calais and Boulogne demonstrated their Emperor's willingness and ability to invade England should the talks break down. St Vincent was confident that British naval supremacy made invasion impossible. To the nervous Cabinet he was simultaneously offensive and reassuring: 'I do not say the French cannot come, I only say they cannot come by sea.'

Nelson was an essential part of that supremacy. Not only his courage and experience were needed. His reputation was part of England's protection. His presence heartened the fleet and un-nerved the enemy. So (as he wrote to Prince William, now Duke of Clarence), he received a 'commission as Commander-in-Chief of a Squadron of Ships and Vessels employed on particular service'. The letter ended on an uncharacteristically humble note 'I feel my ability to render service . . . only in my zeal; in many other respects I am sensible of much deficiency and require that great allowances should be made for me.' Nelson's confidence – not in himself, that was never in doubt, but in the reputation he enjoyed in the Admiralty – had been restored by the last sentence of a letter recently received: 'I need not add how very important it is that the enemy should know *you* are constantly opposed to him.'

The task did not fulfil its romantic promise. It included the recruitment of Sea Fencibles (naval volunteers) and the improvement of shore defences, work which Nelson discharged with some surprise that such duties should be thought sufficiently important to demand his services only three weeks after his return from Copenhagen. In fact the Board of Admiralty was less concerned with the urgency of the work

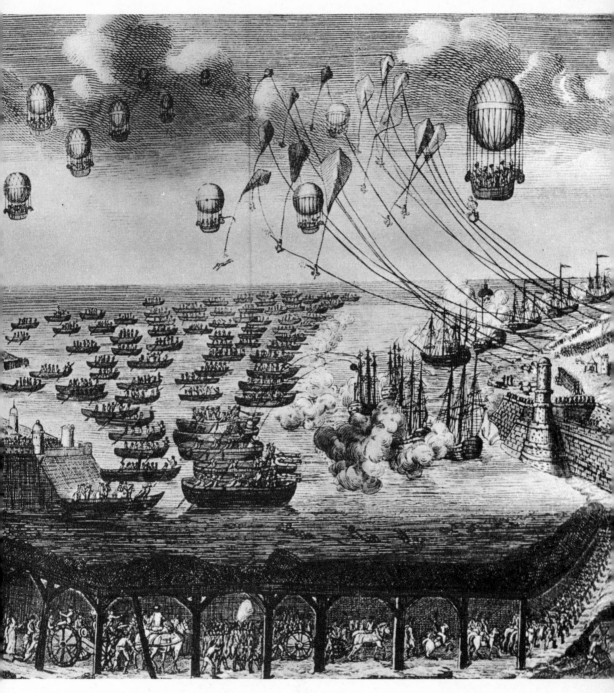

PREVIOUS PAGES Napoleon's
'*Grande Armée*' encamped at
Boulogne in preparation for
the final assault on England.

ABOVE An imaginative plan for the
invasion of England by air, sea and
tunnel submitted to – and rejected
by – Napoleon in 1804.

145

The repulse of the English raid
on Boulogne, August 1804.

than with the necessity to keep Nelson and the Hamiltons apart. The gossip was becoming too much for their lordships. It was tarnishing the reputation of England's authentic hero.

In August even his reputation for seamanship and naval command was questioned. In the middle of August the British attacked Boulogne. Though the invaders were ill-prepared, the defences were not and the invaders were repulsed with many casualties. While Nelson attributed the failure of the expedition to the fact that he had not led it himself, there were those in England anxious to find in him cause for their dissatisfaction. A Mr Hill asked for £100 as the price of the suppression of his analysis of the Boulogne disaster and Nelson's responsibility for it. Nelson refused and the Hill article was added to the list of public criticism.

But there were consolations. Nelson rightly remained the people's hero and official blessing was at last given to his irregular practice of describing himself Duke of Bronte. The Neapolitan title was added to the recently gazetted style 'Lord Nelson of the Nile and of Hilborough in the County of Norfolk' but the old magic of Naples was incapable of re-capture. The Hamiltons made a brief visit to Deal (with the improbable intention of tending the Boulogne casualties) but Nelson was not given leave to accompany them back to London. A letter for 'Mrs Thomson care of Lady Hamilton' followed them two days later:

I came on board but no Emma. No, no my heart will break! I am in silent distraction. The four pictures of Lady Hamilton are hung up but, alas, I have lost the original. But we part only to meet again very soon: it must be, it *shall* be. . . . My dearest wife, how can I bear our separation. . . . I am so low I cannot hold up my head. . . . Love my Horatia and prepare for me the farm.

The farm was a recently acquired estate at Merton near Wimbledon for which Nelson had, with difficulty, paid £9,000. Sir William and Lady Hamilton were installed there to await the return of the hero owner. He arrived on 22 October 1801 temporarily released from service at sea by the Peace of Amiens.

The next eighteen months were probably the most enjoyable period of Nelson's life. His father, reconciled to the irregular union, moved into Merton to pass his declining days with the peculiar trio. After his death in April 1802 (his son, still suffering from constantly recurring fever, was too ill to attend his funeral), Nelson increasingly treated Hamilton

as a father. It seems impossible that Sir William did not realise the abiding relationship between his wife and his host or recognise the real parentage of Horatia. But he did not let it disturb the comfort of his old age. He helped Horatia with her neglected education and explained to Charles Greville (Emma had been his mistress before she was passed on to the Hamilton family), 'I am determined that my quiet shall not be disturbed, let the nonsensical world go on as it will.'

The praise of the world continued to be heaped on Nelson. In July 1802 a West Country excursion turned into a triumphant tour of honour. On 21 July Nelson received the freedom of Oxford, William Hamilton was awarded an honorary doctorate by the University and William Nelson became a Doctor of Divinity. At Blenheim, the next day, the party was offended by being offered only a cold collation rather than lunch with the Duke of Marlborough and left in dudgeon for Gloucester and Ross-on-Wye where the rapturous reception made up for the disappointment at Woodstock.

ABOVE Merton Place –
the Hamiltons' house in
England. Emma talks
to a gardener while Sir
William fishes.
RIGHT Merton Place,
Surrey, by Thomas Baxter
c.1803. The river which
passed the breakfast room
was re-named 'The Nile'.

148

Monmouth celebrated their visit with such a memorable festival that four years later a Nelson Museum was founded in the town to immortalise the hero who had passed that way. Charles Greville arranged a 'festival' at Milford, and Swansea assembled the Mayor and all the Corporation. During the return journey, Monmouth was afforded the rare privilege of two songs from Lady Hamilton, sung at an evening soirée to mark her gratitude for the first visit. Ross-on-Wye built a triumphal arc of flowers. Worcester and Hereford made Nelson a Freeman. In Birmingham ('the toy shop of Europe') Nelson was fêted at the theatre, conducted round innumerable factories and visited Matthew Bolton. Coventry and Warwick lay almost on the natural route to London so both were favoured with a visit. The party returned to Merton, tired in body, exhilarated in spirit and bearing bills for the trip which totalled £481.3.10. Nelson had no idea how they were to be paid.

The winter passed quietly at Merton with Hamilton's health in remorseless deterioration. In early spring, certain of his impending death and absurdly considerate to the end, William Hamilton insisted that he be moved to Piccadilly, determined that a death at Merton would destroy the idyllic atmosphere that Emma and Horatio had created in the house. On 29 March 1803 he composed his Will, leaving Nelson his favourite portrait of his wife. He had two attentive nurses and companions who scarcely left his sick room during the final days. He died on 6 April 1803, in his wife's arms and holding her lover's hand. An extraordinary relationship had ended extraordinarily.

Five weeks after Sir William's death, England was at war with France again. The Peace of Amiens (by which both French and English had been obliged to return virtually all their conquests to the powers from whom they had been taken) had never looked permanent. It collapsed on 18 May 1803. In anticipation of a war renewed, Nelson had been appointed to the Mediterranean fleet two days earlier. At the hour hostilities were resumed, he hoisted his flag as Vice-Admiral of the Blue. In Toulon, Admiral Touche-Treville was taking command of the French fleet at the same moment. Touche-Treville had beaten Nelson at Boulogne in 1802. He was sure that he could do it again in a bigger battle. Fate was not to give him the chance.

Nelson left England with two personal matters unresolved.

LEFT Lord Nelson after Beechey.

151

Money had been scarce for five years. Always conscious of the debt the nation owed to him and never too proud to suggest that it should be repaid, Nelson decided to ask for his dues from a grudging Government and ungrateful Admiralty. Emma (who had been left £800 a year by her husband) seemed to Nelson to be equally neglected by a nation that should have recompensed her for the services she rendered in Naples. Nelson suggested a pension of £1,200 would be appropriate. The Treasury did not agree. His own complaint he laid before Addington. St Vincent and Duncan had been awarded pensions of £3,000 a year, while he − despite the more important victories of Copenhagen and the Nile − got £2,000. Addington was unable or unwilling to help. Nelson changed the grounds for his application from the obligations of gratitude to the demands of stark necessity. He set out a statement of his income and expenditure which purported to show that as things were, he could not live.

The Admiralty remained sceptical − perhaps because the balance sheet was so obviously concocted to add spurious strength to Nelson's case. It argued that Lady Nelson *needed* a separate establishment. It made no mention of the revenue he received from the Bronte estate in Sicily. It also claimed that Fanny received £450 a year. In fact she was paid £400. There was no way in which their lordships could help. Nelson remained worried about money for the rest of his life.

He remained equally concerned about Emma's reputation and with the need to preserve what he still believed to be a general ignorance of the true nature of their relationship. After the christening of Horatia, Lord Nelson and Lady Hamilton performed a bizarre ceremony on the altar steps during which they swore before heaven the innocence of their relationship. As a sign of her piety, he bought a Bible and prayer book for each member of his ship's company: 874 men and boys.

Emma was less sensitive to the need for consciously preserved respectability. There was a brief period of grief − real or artificial − immediately after her husband's death. But within weeks she was singing to entertain her guests and drinking noticeably large quantities of porter. Indeed her capacity was so great, and her ability to remain sober so remarkable, that it was generally supposed that she had the advantage of years of practice.

For the first weeks of his new service, Nelson flew his flag in the *Amphion*. The *Victory* was to be his when Collingwood hauled his down. During the days while Collingwood remained on board the new flagship, Nelson recruited and assembled his personal staff. Most would remain with him until the end: Thomas Hardy (who became Fleet Captain before Trafalgar), John Scott his secretary and Doctor Scott his personal surgeon. On 8 July 1803, the *Amphion* joined the fleet off Toulon. It was to be 'blockading work' again carried out under increasingly difficult circumstances. Nelson had learned the need for fresh food to keep his sailors happy. It was part of the 'Nelson touch' which was proving almost impossible to apply. Even when the *Victory* was restored to him, the fleet moved its base to Sardinia, but it proved no better a source of vegetables and victuals. The weather remained rough and morale seemed likely to fall.

La Touche-Treville remained stubbornly in port until the end of the year. In early 1804 he began to make the occasional sortie towards the British fleet. Nelson was contemptuous of his tactics: 'My friend sometimes plays bo-peep in and out of Toulon like a mouse at the edge of the hole.' In the hope that the French could be lured into the open, most of the British fleet disappeared over the horizon, leaving only a small squadron under Sir Richard Bickerton visible from Toulon. The French remained in port. On 13 June a major sortie was attempted. Nelson (for three weeks a Vice-Admiral of the White, the highest rank he ever held) engaged the enemy on the 14th and drove them back to port.

That was not how La Touche-Treville described the outcome of the battle to his Emperor. To Nelson's chagrin a report reached the fleet that according to the French account of the engagement, the British had run away. The French version was even quoted in some English newspapers and Nelson wrote to brother William vowing revenge: 'You will have seen Monsieur La Touche's letter of how he chased me and how I *ran*. I keep it; and my God if I take him, he shall *eat* it.'

In fact Nelson's strategy was – properly – less bold than his words. In part that was the product of age and experience. The determination to sail towards the sound (or prospect) of gunfire, whatever the wisdom of setting such a course, was no longer his abiding naval characteristic. He had become a sailor of judgment, anxious not to engage the French too close to their shore, where they could find shelter and he could

153

not, and his officers were as often praised for the avoidance of dangerous encounters as they were urged on in the pursuit of glory.

The opportunity to require La Touche-Treville to eat his words never came. He died in August 1804 and was replaced by Admiral Villeneuve. It seemed unlikely that the old enemies would face each other again for some time. Nelson's health had deteriorated again. There were bouts of fever again and a new complication had developed. The head wound received at Cape St Vincent was giving great pain and there was constant concern unless the sight of his good eye should be lost. An application for home leave was granted. It reached Nelson in December 1804.

The news arrived too late. Spain had entered the war a few days earlier and in the face of the new threat Nelson decided that he must remain at his post, a decision which he regarded as typical of his self-sacrificing character and began to regret when he discovered that a new command under Sir John Orde was to be set up west of Gibraltar. Not only honour was at stake. Prize-money was in regular prospect in the waters where Orde was in command. Orde, already rich, was unmoved by the chance. Nelson, frantic about his deteriorating financial situation, was so envious that he made no secret of his resentment of Orde's presence. Relations between the two Admirals so worsened that, three months after Orde's arrival, Nelson began to send dispatches home to London by a route which did not allow his colleague the opportunity of opening them.

On New Year's Day 1805 Villeneuve made his first attempt to run the blockade. The British fleet was, he knew, under strength – denied reinforcement by an Admiralty Board that could find insufficient wood to build new ships. Nelson did not realise that the French had ventured out until seventeen days after they set sail. By the time news of the French flight reached the British Admiral, the attempt to shake free of Nelson had failed and was over. Bad weather had forced the French back into Toulon. Had Villeneuve broken free, he would have made at once for the West Indies, hoping that Nelson would follow there. The French, realising that invasion of Britain was impossible while Nelson patrolled the western Mediterranean, decided that the best tactic was an attempt to lure him three thousand miles from home. If Villeneuve could run and outwit the blockade, he would sail to join the fleets of Admirals Ganteaume and Missiessy in the

Admiral Villeneuve.
Defeated by Nelson at
Aboukir Bay, he became
Commander-in-Chief of the
French Mediterranean
fleet in August 1804.

Caribbean. Nelson would have to follow. At some point the French would double back and mount the invasion of England.

The 1 January attempt to beat the blockade failed because of bad weather. On 30 March, a second attempt to escape succeeded. Once out of Toulon the French fleet, joined by seven more ships of the Napoleonic Navy, sailed due west. Villeneuve reached Martinique on 14 May (after an unhappy six-week journey) with a thousand sick seamen to disembark for rest and recuperation.

When the news of the French escape reached the English fleet, Nelson was immediately certain that they had sailed east towards the Levant. Nelson sailed in what he believed was pursuit. It was not until 6 May – five weeks after the actual escape from Toulon – that the British discovered the real destination of their enemy. Nelson turned west at once and followed his opponent towards the Americas as the French intended that he should.

The first part of the French plan went exactly as Villeneuve had predicted that it would but the outcome of his stratagem was not what he anticipated. The British allowed themselves to be dragged off their proper station and left the Mediterranean virtually free to the French. But what Nelson's fleet lacked in tactical subtlety, it more than made up for in seamanship. It took Villeneuve more than five weeks to reach the West Indies. Nelson did the journey in under three, and he arrived with most of his men fit for immediate battle. By the time Nelson arrived in Barbados, Ganteaume and Missiessy had not joined their fleets to Villeneuve's and the proposed harassment of allied shipping had not begun. Nelson's early arrival prevented it from even starting. Villeneuve set sail at once for Europe, making for the Mediterranean with a much smaller fleet under his command than had been intended in the original plan.

Even with Nelson in the West Indies, Britain was not wholly unprotected. In London the First Lord of the Admiralty realised that if the French doubled back, they would find the path to England undefended. So a fleet, under Cornwallis, was sent to cruise off Brest, and Collingwood's squadron was ordered to patrol within striking distance of Cadiz. Villeneuve's return was confirmed on 22 July when a flotilla under Sir Robert Calder met them in the fog as they sailed hard for El Ferrol. Two French prizes were taken, but the enemy were

Sir William Cornwallis by D. Gardner (above) and Cuthbert, Lord Collingwood by H. Howard (above right). Together they supervised the Cadiz blockade while Nelson returned to England.

never really engaged. Calder sailed home to a severe reprimand. Villeneuve joined with the Ferrol squadron of the Spanish Navy on 2 August. The combined fleets, twenty-nine ships in all, sailed west on 14 August, in search of reinforcements expected daily from the Caribbean. The French were regrouping for a major engagement.

But Villeneuve had still not shaken Nelson off. In fact, the British had discovered the French intention to return within hours of Villeneuve's sailing east. Once again Nelson crossed the Atlantic with a speed that his enemy did not contemplate and could not copy. By the time the French and Spanish captains shook hands off Ferrol, Nelson had been in Gibraltar

157

for several days. The path to London was completely blocked again. The combined fleets were back in the defensive position they had so resented in the winter of 1804. Nelson was a hero once more. The British Minister in Naples spoke for the nation:

Either the distance between the different quarters of the globe were diminished or you have extended the powers of human action. After an unremitting cruise of two long years in the stormy Gulf of Lyons, to have proceeded (without going into port) to Alexandria, from Alexandria to the West Indies, from the West Indies back again to Gibraltar, to have kept your ships afloat, your rigging standing and your crews in health and spirits, is an effort such as never was realised in former times nor, I doubt, will ever again be repeated by any other Admiral.

Nelson returned home, briefly, to enjoy the nation's homage and Emma's affection. While he divided his time between Merton and the Admiralty, Villeneuve continued the run of atrocious luck which, almost as much as Nelson's bravery and brilliance, was to come to characterise the Trafalgar campaign. Exceptional gales blew his West Indian reinforcements off course, so Admirals Allamand and Villeneuve never met. Commanding a fleet much smaller than he planned, against an enemy much larger then he expected, left the French Admiral with virtually no alternative. He returned to Cadiz, where the blockade was immediately renewed by Collingwood and Cornwallis. The mastery of the Channel and the subsequent invasion of England was no longer possible for the French. On 29 August, the *Grande Armée*, encamped at Boulogne in preparation for the final assault, turned its back on England for ever and marched to meet the Austrians at Austerlitz.

Nelson remained on shore for almost a month. On 13 September he left Merton for the last time. Two days later he arrived in Portsmouth and set sail in the *Victory* the same day. As he rowed out to his flagship towards its cheering crew, he turned to Hardy: 'I had their huzzas before, I have their hearts now.' His love for the Navy, and the Navy's infatuation with him, had been reborn. The pursuit of duty and daring that he had urged on his sailors, by example and exhortation, was now established faith. The vanity, the courage, the mysticism and the determination that made up Nelson's character had suffused the fleet and prepared it for Britain's greatest victory at sea. And he knew it. On 25 September, well under way, he wrote home to Emma: 'I am anxious to join the fleet, for it would add to my grief if any other man was to give them the Nelson touch, which WE say is warranted never to fail.'

He joined the fleet on 28 September and became immediately aware of how much the Nelson touch was needed. Collingwood was too much of a formal disciplinarian to be loved by his sailors. Robert Calder, his second-in-command, was preoccupied with the fear that he would shortly be recalled. Officially, the criticism of his conduct on 22 July had not reached him. But he suspected that disciplinary action would not be long delayed. The fleet needed something to improve its morale. Nelson's arrival provided it. 'I believe', he wrote home, 'my arrival was most welcome, not only to the Commanders of the Fleet, but to almost every individual in it.' His judgment was being confirmed by the Captains, as they noted in their logs and private diaries. Captain Duff in the *Mars* recorded: 'He is so good and pleasant that we all wish to do what he likes, without any kind of orders.' In the *Donegal*, Captain Malcolm wrote a simple single sentence: 'Nelson is the man to love.'

'The Nelson touch' had always had its practical side – it was concerned as much with nations as with romance, with conditions as well as courage. Nelson found the fleet bored and restless, so he devised a scheme which would both keep the ships' companies employed and fire their imagination. The ships under his command would all be painted 'Mediterranean style', like the *Victory*; black hulls with yellow bands around the ships along the lines of the port-holes. The port-hole covers were painted black so that, when they were closed, the whole hull gave a black and yellow chess-board effect. The men painted furiously, but when the day's painting was over they relaxed in conditions less severe than those recently imposed on them by Admiral Collingwood.

Robert Calder was called home, but sailed for England in the ninety-gun *Prince of Wales* not the frigate which the Admiralty had suggested. The ship was desperately needed by the fleet, but Nelson decided to offer Calder a special courtesy to soften the blow of his recall. The gesture enthused the fleet. The officers, grateful for his consideration to a fallen colleague, were flattered by Nelson's decision to discuss his battle plan with them. By the standards of the time, it was an extraordinary gesture of humility. When the 'Memorandum of 9 October' was issued as orders for the eventual fight, it was a summary of the 'band of brothers' discussion.

Nelson, confident of his own ability, was equally confident in the ability of his officers. Indeed he had no doubts about the general superiority of British seamen, British seamanship and British ships. His confidence was so real and so overwhelming that it was transmitted to the men who served and sailed under him. They believed that they were as magnificent as Nelson believed them to be, and as a result expanded their abilities and increased their courage to a point where it, at least, began to match Nelson's expectations.

Nelson believed that his arrival affected the fleet 'like an electric shock'. Certainly the special powers with which he believed he could imbue his sailors needed to work quickly, for most officers serving under him were neither veterans of previous long campaigns nor old compatriots who could quickly re-create the old relationship. Only eight of his captains had served with him before and of those only Hardy and Berry had been with him since 1803. Only six had been in command of a ship for more than two years. Only five had commanded a ship of the line in battle.

The battle plan that came out of the 'band of brothers' deliberation was simple enough. The fleet would be divided into two squadrons, one surrounding and destroying the enemy rear, the other first containing the van and then destroying the centre. The overall plan was no more than that. Every captain knew that when the battle came, the real orders of the day would simply require him to place his ship alongside the enemy and capture and destroy as much as was possible. The essence of the *Memorandum* was that the strategy reflected the opinion of every captain. The essence of the strategy was that it could not have been more simple.

As the British fleet grew more confident and more carefully prepared for battle, Villeneuve's misfortunes multiplied. Napoleon and Decrès, his Navy Minister, judged the situation from Paris – and continually underestimated Nelson's strength. Villeneuve, actually in sight of the British fleet, took a more realistic view. The French Commander was certainly no coward. His philosophy was typified by the message he signalled to his ships on the morning of the battle: 'The Captain who is not in action is not at his post.' But because of Napoleon's constant miscalculation, he was constantly represented as the Admiral who was reluctant to fight despite the almost certain prospect of victory.

160

Vice-Admiral Sir Robert Calder failed fully to engage Villeneuve's fleet when it returned from the West Indies in July 1805.

On 15 September Villeneuve was ordered to enter the Mediterranean at the first opportunity, and carry troops to Naples. His orders ended with a curt postscript which revealed Napoleon's ignorance of the true balance of naval power: 'Our intention is that whenever you meet the enemy in inferior force you will attack them without hesitation and obtain a decision against them.' Villeneuve remained realistically sceptical and Napoleon, certain that it was cowardice rather than caution that kept his Admiral in port, determined to replace him. However, Vice-Admiral Rosily was appointed as his successor – a man with a reputation for such dash and daring that for *him* Napoleon thought an injunction to prudence was appropriate. How Rosily would have commanded the French fleet remains a mystery. He was a 'traveller of quality' and took ten days to make slow and stately progress

England expects every Man to d

LORD NELSON explaining to the Officers the PLAN of ATTA

V. Adml. Lord Nelson
Captn. T. M. Hardy
Mr. Scott Secy.
V. Adml. Collingwood
Captn. Rotherham
R. Adml. Lord Northesk
Captn. Bullen
Captn. Sir Ed. Berry

Captn. Bayntun
Captn. Codrington
Captn. J. Cooke
Captn. Conn
Captn. H. Digby
Captn. Duff
Captn. Durham
Captn. Freemantle

NAMES of the GALLANT HEROES who Commanded on the 21st. Octr. 1805.

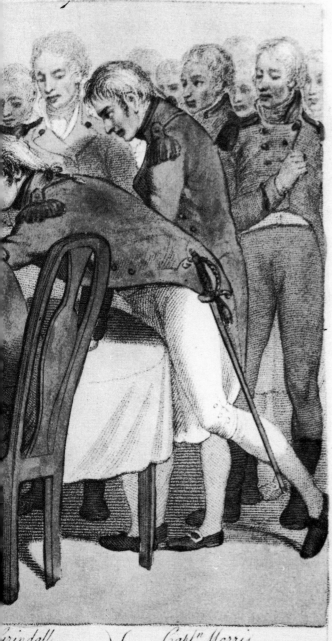

* ous to the* **BATTLE of TRAFALGAR.**

Rindall
argood

Hope
Hervey
ing
r F. Laforey
Hoorsem

Captⁿ Morris
Captⁿ Mansfield
Capt^r I. Pellew
Capt^r Rutherford
Capt^r Ridmill
Captⁿ Tyler
Lieu^t I. Pilford (acting)
Lieu^t I. Stockham (do

Lord Nelson explains the plan of attack
to 'the gallant heroes' of 21 October 1805.

from Madrid to Cadiz. By the time he arrived, the battle was over.

If Napoleon was anxious to see the French fleet at sea, Nelson was even more so. By early October he felt confident of his ability to destroy the French and began to offer every inducement to them to give battle. The blockade continued and essential supplies were scarce in Cadiz. That was the stick. The carrot was supplied by the pretence that the English fleet was a good deal smaller than its actual strength. Instead of lying at anchor ten or fifteen miles from the harbour mouth, Nelson rode out the rougher waters forty to fifty miles from shore. His frigates gave him daily reconnaissance reports on the shape and size of the enemy fleet, whose commander was never allowed to see his adversary.

Battle could not be long delayed. It was like the old glory days of St Vincent and the Nile. The choice between laurel and cypress was in prospect again and the prospect was met with rejoicing: 'I verily believe that the country will soon be put to some expense for my account, either a monument or a new pension and honours, for I have not the very smallest doubt that a very few days, almost hours, will put us in Battle.'

He was right. On 18 October, reports reached Villeneuve that four British ships had sailed eastwards. In the belief that the British ships were scattered (and anxious for some action before Rosily arrived), he decided on prompt action. The following day seven ships of the line and three frigates under Rear-Admiral Magon left Cadiz. Almost at once the wind dropped and the becalmed ships were spotted by Captain Blackwood in the *Euryalus*. The element of surprise was lost, but Villeneuve was committed to action. The rest of his fleet prepared to sail out at 7 a.m. on 20 October.

At noon, Villeneuve ordered his fleet to form into three columns, but bad weather and poor seamanship made the manoeuvre difficult. By 4 p.m., when the wind changed direction, the Combined Fleet was still not in the prescribed order of battle and eighteen British ships of the line were sighted to the south-south-west. At once Villeneuve changed his plan. The fleet were ordered to form a single line of battle, thus (in theory) presenting the maximum fire power to the enemy. In fact, the line was never formed. Throughout the night, every effort was made to pull the fleet into the formation Villeneuve required. Every effort failed.

The news that Villeneuve 'had come out' re-awoke in Nelson all the old prophetic premonitions of death. He discounted the possibility of losing a leg, but contemplated the prospect of losing his life. He would, he announced over dinner, prefer to be buried in St Paul's rather than Westminster Abbey. The Abbey's foundations lay in marshy ground and his body would soon rot. In the drier soil of St Paul's, it would last for ever.

Throughout the day, the British stood ten miles to windward of the Combined Fleet. Blackwood in the *Euryalus* sailed to within three miles of Villeneuve and kept Nelson in constant touch with the enemy's position and apparent capabilities. The British fleet were in the position their Admiral had determined. Unlike the French and Spaniards they had mastered the squalls and the changing wind. A battle was now certain. On the night of 20 October, Nelson spoke to his Midshipmen: 'Tomorrow I will do that which will give you younger gentlemen something to talk and think about for the rest of your lives.'

7
Trafalgar
1805

AT DAWN ON THE MORNING of Monday 21 October 1805, the British fleet stood nine miles to windward of the combined navies of France and Spain. As the light broke, Nelson could see the Combined Fleet silhouetted against the horizon – thirty-three ships of the line, five frigates and two brigs. His command was smaller – twenty-seven ships of the line, five frigates, a schooner and a cutter. If the odds were against him, the auguries were favourable. It was the day of the Burnham Thorpe fair and the anniversary of Captain Suckling's memorable engagement. The Nelsons of Norfolk had always regarded 21 October as a day of celebration and victory.

Soon after 6 a.m. Nelson gave the order for the formation of two columns. The first fifteen ships of the line were led by Collingwood in the *Royal Sovereign*. The second column was led by Nelson in the *Victory*. In the belief that Villeneuve would shirk battle and attempt to return to the sanctuary of Cadiz, the British fleet sailed north-west. Had Nelson's judgment been wrong, the columns would have had to swing south-west to intercept the Combined Fleet as it sailed down the west of Spain. That adjustment would not have been impossible, but the *October Memorandum* which planned for Nelson's smaller squadron to strike at the head of the French line could have been carried out only if one of the British columns had cut through the other. British seamanship might have made both complicated manœuvres simultaneously possible. As it turned out, neither was necessary. Villeneuve realised that his retreat was cut off and that he would have to fight his way into Cadiz. But he was equally sure that it was impossible to avoid the British by running south. A battle was certain in whatever direction he sailed. So he turned for home. Nelson's luck or judgment held. The two British columns sailed smoothly on towards the Combined Fleet in exactly the formation they had decided on 9 October. Every officer knew exactly how the battle should go.

Villeneuve made the signal to turn back north at 8 a.m. His fleet was already in disorder, its morale low and its ships badly prepared for battle. The sudden change of plans, and the prospect of the complicated manœuvre it entailed, was accepted with either gloomy resignation or resentful disbelief. Commander Churruca, Captain of the Spanish *San Juan Nepomuceno*, which had suddenly become not the vanguard but the rear ship in the column, had no doubt what the new

PREVIOUS PAGES Trafalgar. The *Redoutable* about to surrender. The British victory is complete.

168

order meant. 'The fleet is doomed', he said. 'The French Admiral does not understand his business. He has compromised us all.'

The Combined Fleet took a long time turning, improving Nelson's prospects of interception well outside Cadiz. Even when the exercise was complete, the column was scattered with a gap so great between the rear and the centre that, in fact, Villeneuve had formed not one column but two. Four hours later, the confusion continued. At noon, the enemy line still appeared to Collingwood 'a crescent convexing to leeward'.

In contrast, the British fleet was in a state of confident anticipation. Nelson was in 'the taut, omniscient state common to him on such occasions'. He was, as always at the moment of battle, preparing for death and immortality. A codicil was added to his Will. Blackwood and Hardy witnessed and signed the document written on 'October the twenty-first, one thousand, eight hundred and five, then in sight of the Combined Fleets of France and Spain, distant about ten miles'. In fact it was less part of a Will than a manifesto constructed to advance Emma Hamilton's claim to a public pension. The reasons he advanced to justify her claim are more of a credit to Nelson's emotions than to his logic or memory:

Whereas the eminent services of Emma Hamilton, widow of the Right Honorable Sir William Hamilton, have been at the very greatest service to our King and Country, to my knowledge without her receiving any reward from either our King or Country, first, that she obtained the King of Spain's letters, in 1796, to his brother, the King of Naples, acquainting him, of his intention to declare war against England, from which letters the Ministry sent out orders to the then Sir John Jervis, to strike a stroke, if opportunity offered, against either the Arsenals of Spain, or her Fleets. That neither of these was done was not the fault of Lady Hamilton. The opportunity might have been offered. Secondly, the British Fleet under my command, could never have returned the second time to Egypt, had not Lady Hamilton's influence with the Queen of Naples caused letters to be wrote to the Governor of Syracuse, that he was to encourage the Fleet being supplied with everything, should they put into any port in Sicily. We put into Syracuse and received every supply, went to Egypt, and destroyed the French Fleet.

Could I have rewarded these services, I would not now call upon my Country; but as that has not been in my power, I leave Emma, Lady Hamilton, therefore, a legacy to my King and Country, that they will give her an ample provision to maintain her rank in life. I also leave to the beneficence of my Country my adopted daughter, Horatia Nelson Thompson; and I desire she will use in future the name of Nelson only.

These are the only favours I ask of my King and Country at this moment when I am going to fight their Battle. May God bless my King and Country, and all those who I hold dear. My relations it is needless to mention – they will, of course, be amply provided for.

Having witnessed the Will, Blackwood urged Nelson to conduct the battle from the safety of the *Euryalus*. Nelson refused. At nine o'clock he changed into a battered, but be-ribboned, dress uniform and, accompanied by his four frigate Captains, toured the *Victory*. The crew seemed eager for battle. Their spirit only partly confirmed Nelson's judgment of British seamanship. At least half of them were foreign sea-men, recruited to fill the gaps left by the failure of 'Hearts of Oak' to join the Navy. Despite the press-gang, the fleet was chronically undermanned. The prospect of serving under Nelson had attracted two hundred volunteers to swell the ship's company. But the *Victory* was still short of its full complement despite the Frenchmen, Spaniards, Italians, Hindus, Norwegians, Portuguese, Swiss, Dutchmen and Americans who had been recruited in the hope of plugging the gaps.

The tour completed, Nelson 'ate a bit of raw pork and half a pint of wine' as the *Victory* was being prepared for battle – loose equipment lashed down, deck space cleared and the galley made ready for the receipt of wounded. At eleven o'clock, Nelson went to his cabin for the last time and wrote his final prayer:

May the Great God, whom I worship, grant to my Country and for the benefit of Europe in general a great and glorious victory; and may no misconduct in anyone tarnish it; and may humanity after victory be the predominant feature of the British Fleet. For myself, individually, I commit my life to Him who made me, and may His blessing light upon my endeavours for serving my Country faithfully. To Him I resign myself and the just cause which is entrusted to me to defend. Amen. Amen. Amen.

The prayer written as well as said (Nelson was always conscious of his obligations to posterity), the Commander-in-Chief returned to the poop deck. In order to ensure that the column would strike at the van of the Combined Fleet, course was adjusted by twenty degrees to the north. Action was about

At nine o'clock on the morning of the battle, Nelson changed into dress uniform and toured the *Victory*.

Nelson's diary –
Monday 25
October 1805.
The final entry.

to begin. The *Victory*'s band struck up *Rule Britannia* and
Britons Strike Home. Nelson decided 'to amuse the fleet' and
asked Captain Pasco to make the signal 'England Confides
That Every Man Will Do His Duty.' Either Pasco or Blackwood reminded Nelson that the signal code did not contain a
single flag that represented the word 'confides'. The expression of confidence by so archaic a verb would have required
the word to be spelled out on the signal mast, letter by letter.
There was, however, a single flag to express expectation.
Believing the message to be unchanged by the alteration,
Nelson agreed to an amended signal, 'England Expects That
Every Man Will Do His Duty.' It was received in the Fleet
with a mixture of surprise and triumph – surprise from those
who believed 'expects' to imply a degree of uncertainty about
their likely performance, and triumph by those who accepted
the message in the terms which Nelson intended. With the

172

to My Country and for the benefit of Europe in general a great and Glorious Victory, and may no misconduct in any one tarnish it and may humanity after Victory be the predominant feature in the British fleet, For myself individually I commit my life t Him who made

me and may his blessing light upon my endeavours for serving my country faithfully, to Him I resign myself and the Just cause which is entrusted to me to Defend Amen. amen. amen

advantage of hind sight Napoleon had no doubt what the signal meant. In 1806 every ship in the French navy was embellished, on his instruction, with the inscription 'La France Compte que Chacun Fera son Devoir'.

The next signal to be hoisted – Number 16 – had a single and certain meaning, 'Close upon the enemy and begin action.' Lieutenant Nicholas, a Marine Officer on the *Belleisle*, described the men who were about to engage the enemy: 'Some were stripped to the waist; some had bared their necks and arms; others had tied a handkerchief round their heads and all seemed eagerly to await the order to engage.' On board the *Royal Sovereign*, Admiral Collingwood recommended First Lieutenant Clavell to change his knee-boots for shoes and stockings as 'They are so much more manageable for the surgeons.'

At a quarter to twelve, the Combined Fleet received the

Captain Blackwood, commander of the frigates at Trafalgar who probably suggested a simplification of Nelson's signal to the fleet. 'Expects' replaced 'confides'.

order from Villeneuve to open fire as soon as the enemy were within range. Collingwood's column was the first within range. By accident or design, the *Royal Sovereign* had deviated from the original plan and was closing with the sixteenth enemy ship from the rear – not the twelfth as the *October Memorandum* had stipulated. Nelson, according to plan not in a position to engage until after Collingwood was locked with the Combined Fleet, regretted missing even the first moments of the battle – 'See how that noble fellow Collingwood takes his ship into action, how I envy him!'

The *Fougueux* opened fire on the *Royal Sovereign* at two minutes to twelve. At noon, Collingwood's flagship, the *Belleisle*, the *Mars* and the *Tonnant* were in range of six ships of the Combined Fleet and under heavy bombardment. At first it was impossible for Collingwood to return fire as he was sailing directly towards the enemy. On board the *Royal*

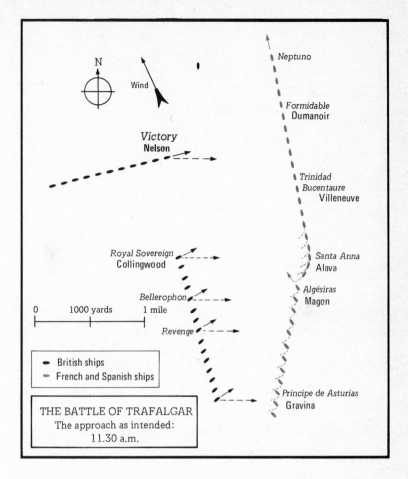

THE BATTLE OF TRAFALGAR
The approach as intended:
11.30 a.m.

Sovereign, one sailor recorded his feelings: 'They fought us pretty tight for French and Spaniards . . . to tell you the truth of it, when the game began I wished myself at Warnborough with my plough again – but when they had given us one duster, and I find myself snug and tight, I bid fear kiss my bottom and set to in good and earnest.'

At eight minutes past twelve, the *Royal Sovereign* passed through the enemy line and fired a crippling broadside into the *Santa Anna*. Three minutes later the *Belleisle* was in the enemy line and, together with the *Royal Sovereign*, was engaging the *Santa Anna*, the *Fougueux* and the *Indomptable*. Collingwood's column (which had half turned so as to approach the enemy in a line which faced due north and ran from north-west to south-east) sailed so close and tight that half of its ships were in action by half past twelve. The French line was completely broken. The British ships, although under continuous and heavy fire, penetrated the enemy line and began to take on the rear of the column, ship by ship. Midshipman Roberts, who watched the engagement from aboard the *Victory*, recalled: 'It was a glorious sight to see the Royal Sovereign commence action. . . . She fired a most tremendous broadside to begin with, but we did not see her but a very short time, she was soon involved in smoke and the flash of guns made it appear awfully grand.'

The *Victory* came under enemy fire twelve minutes later than the *Royal Sovereign*. Initially, Nelson sailed towards the head of Villeneuve's column as if to cut it off from Cadiz, but he suddenly altered course and headed for the centre of the Combined Fleet and the general direction of Villeneuve in the *Bucentaure*, although neither Nelson nor Hardy had recognised the French flagship. For a time, Nelson allowed a number of his ships to precede him into battle. However, when the column was within minutes of engaging the enemy, he increased sail and called out to the *Téméraire*, 'I'll thank you Captain Harvey to keep in your proper station, which is *astern* of the *Victory*.'

The Combined Fleet opened fire on the *Victory* at ten minutes past twelve. The first shot struck the British flagship five minutes later. As Nelson sailed directly at the French column it was impossible to return the enemy fire, although he was under continuous heavy bombardment. Before the *Victory* fired a shot, fifty British sailors were dead, the mizzenmast was down and the wheelhouse shot away. For the rest of the battle the ship was steered by the tiller, operated by hand from the gunroom, 'The First Lieutenant, John Quilliam, and Master, Thomas Atkinson, relieving each other at this duty.'

The *Victory* returned fire at twenty-four minutes past twelve, but was still not in a position to inflict any serious damage on the enemy. Yet, despite the heavy damage she was receiving, the *Victory* continued to spearhead the inexorable British advance. At half past twelve, the *Victory* ensured the division of the enemy column by ramming the *Redoutable* and seconds later, hit the *Bucentaure* with a broadside fired from only thirty yards. The British had split the Combined Fleet in a second place. Villeneuve decided that only by bringing his van to the support of his centre could his column be preserved and saved. But the signal he made to his fleet was wildly imprecise and did no more than order all captains

The battle of Trafalgar
by Nicholas Pocock.
The *Victory* breaks
the French line.

178

LEFT Captain Sir Thomas Hardy
by an unknown artist.

BELOW The battle of Trafalgar
by Turner.

to make every effort to engage the enemy. Admiral Dumanoir at the head of the column had no idea what the order meant, so he did nothing.

Although Villeneuve feared that the battle was lost, on board the *Victory* many seamen and marines must have thought that fortune favoured the French. The cockpit, to which the dead and dying were taken, was (according to the Ship's Chaplain) 'like a butcher's shambles'. At a quarter past one, unable to stand the sight of death and mutilation any longer, he ran out on to the deck where he met Captain Hardy who, a moment earlier, had felt the buckle shot from his shoe by musket fire. As the Chaplain approached, Hardy turned towards him. But it was not the distressed Chaplain that caught the Captain's attention. Nelson was on his knees with the finger tips of his left hand just touching the deck. As Hardy rushed towards him, he looked up and said 'They have done for me Hardy. . . . My backbone is shot through.' Nelson had been hit by a single musket shot fired from the rigging of the *Redoutable*, virtually the last action of a ship irreparably damaged.

After covering Nelson's face and medals with handkerchiefs – so as to avoid the consternation that would have spread through the ship at the news of the Admiral's fatal wound – Hardy ordered three seamen to carry him to the cockpit below. Dr Beatty, the ship's surgeon, had fifty sick men waiting attention. This time, unlike the Nile, Nelson was in no condition to insist that he wait his turn for attention, but as Beatty and Burke, the ship's Purser, carried him to a berth, he told them, 'You can do nothing for me. I have but a short time to live. My back is shot through.'

Nelson continued to explain that the wound was mortal. He begged of Beatty, 'Remember me to Lady Hamilton! Remember me to Horatia! Remember me to all my friends! Doctor, remember me to Mr Rose; tell him I have left a will, and left Lady Hamilton and Horatia to my country.' The surgeon began to examine the wound. Nelson described his symptoms. He had no feeling in the lower part of his body, breathing was painful and difficult and he felt 'a gush of blood every minute within his breast'. Beatty concluded that the musket-ball was lodged in Nelson's spine. That in itself suggested that the wound would be fatal. A rapidly weakening pulse confirmed the diagnosis. He told Hardy, Burke and the second surgeon, Scott, that Nelson was dying.

Nelson himself had no doubt about his condition. He
contradicted every suggestion that he would recover: 'It is
nonsense, Mr Burke, to suppose I can live', and began to call
for Captain Hardy. 'Will no one bring Hardy to me? He must
be killed.' A boy was sent to look for the Flag Captain. The
boy returned with the message that 'Circumstances respecting the fleet require Captain Hardy's presence on deck' but
that he would 'avail himself of the first favourable moment to
visit his Lordship.'

When he arrived, Nelson began, at once, to cross-examine
him: 'Well, Hardy, how goes the battle? How goes the day
with us?'

'Very well, my Lord', Hardy assured him. 'We have got
twelve or fourteen of the enemy's ships in our possession, but
five of their van have tacked, and show an intention of bearing

'The Death of Nelson' from the Royal Gallery, House of Lords. A heroic (and highly inaccurate) representation of the final moments.

down upon the *Victory*. I have, therefore, called two or three of our fresh ships round us, and have no doubt of giving them a drubbing.'

'I hope none of our ships have struck, Hardy.'

'No, my Lord. There is no fear of that.'

'I am a dead man, Hardy. I am going fast – it will be over with me soon. Come nearer to me. Pray let my dear Lady Hamilton have my hair, and all things belonging to me.'

Beatty decided that he must confirm Nelson's own judgment that he had only hours to live. 'My Lord', he said, 'unhappily for our Country nothing further can be done for you.' Nelson accepted the prognosis with calm resignation: 'I know. I feel something rising in my breast which tells me that I am gone. God be praised. I have done my duty.'

Fifty minutes after his first visit, Hardy returned to the

183

cockpit. He shook Nelson's hand and congratulated him upon 'a brilliant victory which is complete'. He was unable to say precisely how many ships of the Combined Fleet were destroyed or captured, but was certain that fourteen or fifteen had surrendered.

'That is well', Nelson replied, 'but I bargained for twenty.'

But he developed a sudden agitation. 'Anchor, Hardy, Anchor!'

'I suppose, my Lord, Admiral Collingwood will now take upon himself the direction of affairs.' In fact, Hardy had told Collingwood that his commander was mortally wounded and incapable of directing the battle. But Nelson was not yet ready to relinquish his responsibilities.

'Not while I live, I hope, Hardy! No. Do *you* anchor Hardy.'

'Shall I make the signal, Sir?'

'Yes, for if I live, I'll anchor.'

Surgeon Beatty, who wrote the account of the final moments and last conversations, noted that Nelson had no doubt 'that in a few minutes he should be no more'. He had a dying request.

'Don't throw me overboard, Hardy.'

Hardy was almost too moved to reply. After a brief pause he gave the assurance. 'Oh no, certainly not.'

The dying moments, Beatty recorded with what he later claimed to be absolute accuracy:

'Then' replied his Lordship 'you know what to do. And take care of my dear Lady Hamilton, Hardy, take care of poor Lady Hamilton. Kiss me Hardy.'

The Captain now knelt down and kissed his cheek, when his Lordship said 'Now I am satisfied – thank God I have done my duty.'

Captain Hardy stood a minute or two in silent contemplation. He knelt down again and kissed his Lordship's forehead.

His Lordship said 'Who is that?'

The Captain answered 'It is Hardy', to which his Lordship replied 'God bless you Hardy.'

Hardy now withdrew a second and last time. Nelson asked to be turned on his right side and then said:

'I wish I had not left the deck, for I shall soon be gone.'

Doctor Scott, still massaging Nelson's neck and providing constant drinks of lemonade, was the recipient of the last confidence: 'Doctor, I have *not* been a *great* sinner.' He paused and then continued. 'Remember, that I leave Lady

'The Death of Nelson' by A. W. Devis. 'I am a dead man, Hardy, I am going fast – it will be over with me soon.'

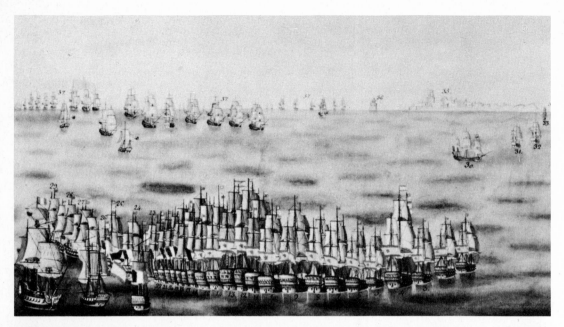

Spanish paintings of
the battle of Trafalgar.

Hamilton and my daughter Horatia as a legacy to my Country – and never forget Horatia.'

His last words were the message he had repeated over and over again during the last agony: 'Thank God I have done my duty.' Then the pulse grew weaker, the temperature fell further and the final paralysis set in. At half past four, precisely, Dr Beatty announced that Vice-Admiral Horatio Nelson was dead.

Nelson lay dying in the cockpit of the *Victory* for well over three hours. During that time the battle of Trafalgar had raged on, with the British fleet initially under the direction of Captain Hardy and finally under the command of Admiral Collingwood. In fact, the pattern of the battle had been determined from the moment when the *Victory* made the second breach in the Combined Fleet's column. As the British sailed towards the enemy, unable to open fire, the issue was theoretically in doubt. Once they had survived Villeneuve's bombardment without being deflected from their line of sail, the odds were in Nelson's favour. As soon as both Collingwood's and Nelson's columns had penetrated the Franco-Spanish formation, the battle was actually won for Britain. With the Combined Fleet split into three desperate and isolated pieces, victory was certain for the navy which had superior seamanship and the most accomplished gunnery. There was no doubt which navy that was.

At twenty minutes to two, the *Bucentaure*, the French flagship, received its final bombardment from the *Conqueror*. Five minutes later, its colours were struck. The Captain of the *Bucentaure* agreed that there was no alternative: 'Our ship was so riddled that it seemed to be no more than a mass of wreckage.' By two o'clock both the *Redoutable* and the *Fougueux* fell to the British *Téméraire* and the issue was virtually decided. The French flagship and two of Villeneuve's most powerful ships of the line had fallen. As a result the French were becoming increasingly outnumbered in the centre.

At the moment of the *Bucentaure*'s surrender, Admiral Dumanoir finally gave the order for the van to turn and sail to the assistance of the centre of the column. Hardy, recognising their intention, ordered the English column to reform in preparation for the new onslaught. Once again, British seamanship won the day. The regrouping was carried out so swiftly – and the van of the Combined Fleet turned with such cumberous uncertainty – that by the time Admiral Dumanoir's ships had come to the rescue of the centre of the Combined Fleet's column, the British had regrouped and were ready to meet them. The *Leviathan, Conqueror, Neptune, Ajax, Agamemnon* and *Britannia* formed a rough line sailing north-west and in the direct path of the returning Dumanoir. Once again, the Combined Fleet was split by the British, the eight ships dividing into three groups. Hardy first picked off two of the enemy, then concentrated on three more and finally turned his attention to the remaining three.

At the rear of the Combined Fleet's column, the battle furiously continued. Captain Duff of the *Mars* was killed at the same moment Nelson was hit, and his ship, like the *Royal Sovereign*, severely damaged, began to drift out of control. But they were the only major casualties in the British fleet. Collingwood's column had achieved its objective of getting almost within grappling distance of the enemy. The short-range bombardment of the hull-to-hull battle produced enormous casualties on both sides. But it suited the British who were able to sustain rapid fire and willing to continue the fight despite the carnage on their decks. At twenty minutes past two, the *Santa Anna* with Admiral Alava seriously wounded and three hundred bodies piled between gunwales, lost its mizzenmast. Its colours were struck, and defeat for the Combined Fleet became as assured at the rear of the column as it was certain in the middle.

The *Mars*, swinging towards the head of the Combined Fleet's column, joined the *Victory* and opened fire on the van at about three o'clock. An hour later only ten or twelve ships of the Franco-Spanish fleet remained in battle. From then on, it was simply a mopping-up operation. At half past four, Admiral Dumanoir gave his squadron the signal to disengage and escape south-south-west. Admiral Gravina, aboard the *Principe de Asturias*, signalled to the rest of the Combined Fleet that they should make for Cadiz. As the battle ended, the prizes taken by the British Navy drifted into a ring around the *Victory* as if attracted by a magnetic force. The log of the British flagship recorded the effective end of the battle: 'Partial firing continued until 4.30 when victory having been reported to the Rt Hon. Lord Viscount Nelson, K.B. and Commander-in-Chief, he died of his wound.'

At half past five the *Intrepide*, the last ship of the Combined

Trafalgar, detail of a painting
by Turner: Nelson wounded
at the moment of victory.

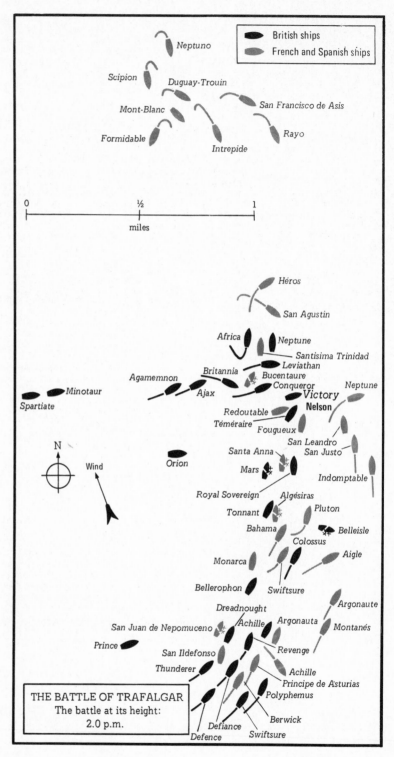

British ships
French and Spanish ships

Neptuno

Scipion

Duguay-Trouin

San Francisco de Asis

Mont-Blanc

Rayo

Formidable

Intrepide

0   ½   1
miles

Héros

San Agustin

Africa   Neptune

Santisima Trinidad

Britannia   Leviathan

Agamemnon   Bucentaure

Conqueror   Neptune

Ajax   Victory

Nelson

Minotaur

Spartiate   Redoutable   San Leandro

Téméraire   San Justo

Fougueux

N

Indomptable

Wind   Orion

Santa Anna

Mars

Royal Sovereign   Algésiras

Tonnant   Pluton

Bahama   Belleisle

Colossus

Aigle

Monarca

Bellerophon   Swiftsure

Argonaute

Dreadnought   Montanés

San Juan de Nepomuceno   Achille   Argonauta

Prince   Revenge

San Ildefonso   Achille

Thunderer   Principe de Asturias

Polyphemus

THE BATTLE OF TRAFALGAR
The battle at its height:
2.0 p.m.

Defiance   Berwick

Defence   Swiftsure

The battle of Trafalgar over, the damaged *Victory* is towed towards Gibraltar.

Fleet to abandon the struggle, struck its colours after what one British observer called 'one of the most gallant defences I ever saw'. It had been a day of great gallantry on both sides of the battle, and a battle in which each side was anxious to acknowledge the achievements of the enemy. As the *Intrepide* surrendered, the *Achille* blew up. Lieutenant Nicholas of the *Belleisle* recalled: 'The *Achille* had burnt to the water's edge, with the tricolour ensign still displayed, about a mile from us, and our tenders and boats were using every effort to save the poor fellows who had so gloriously defended her – but only two hundred and fifty were rescued and she blew up with a tremendous explosion.'

Admiral Gravina gathered together eleven ships of the Combined Fleet and made for Cadiz; the *Principe de Asturias*, unable to proceed under her own sail, was towed to safe harbour. Admiral Dumanoir in the *Formidable* led four ships to the south-west. Eighteen vessels of the Combined Fleet had struck their colours – only two less than the number Nelson had hoped to capture – while the British had not lost a single vessel.

Even that did not complete the French humiliation. On 4 November, a British squadron under Sir Richard Strachan captured the four ships which Dumanoir hoped to lead to safety. Captain Charles Paget believed that the postscript to

This ALLEGORICAL PRINT is by permission dedicated to the Right Honble. the LORDS COMMISSIONERS of the ADMIRALTY.

the battle made 'the smash complete'. In fact it was more complete than an Englishman could have realised in early November 1805. Of the eight ships of the Combined Fleet which limped into Cadiz harbour, only the *Neptune* and the *Montanez* were ever fit to sail again. Of the men under Villeneuve's command, 4,530 were killed in battle including Rear-Admiral Magon and nine ships' captains. The wounded numbered 3,573, among them Rear-Admirals Cisneros, Alava and Gravina and ten ships' captains. Villeneuve was captured together with several hundreds of the men who served under him. By comparison, British casualties were light – 449 men killed and 1,214 wounded. The death roll throughout Nelson's entire fleet was less than the tally of dead in the *Redoutable* alone.

The size – indeed the fact – of the victory was directly attributable to the quality of seamanship in the fleet under Nelson's command. As the two columns approached the Combined Fleet, both had come under heavy gunfire which they were unable either to return or avoid. Yet they had sailed unhesitatingly onward with neither the spirit nor the efficiency of their crews impaired. That was a tribute to the courage of Nelson's sailors and to the faith they had in themselves, not least because of the faith Nelson had in them.

Once the British fleet had sailed into the enemy's column or manœuvred alongside the French and Spanish ships, they opened up a barrage of destructive cannon fire that the gunners of the Combined Fleet could not match. The gun-layers in the British men-of-war could re-charge faster and aim straighter than any fighting sailors in the world. It was their trade. Thanks to the standard upon which Nelson insisted, they were superb tradesmen. They were encouraged to improve their craft by constant practice. They were scrupulous in the care of their cannon, their powder and their shot. They felt that Nelson was equally anxious to keep them in fighting trim. Despite the press-gang, the history of summary justice and exemplary punishment and the gulf which permanently separated the Ward Room from the lower deck, Nelson had created a professional navy. At Trafalgar it won a professional victory.

Nelson himself never doubted the outcome, though, when the battle began, the odds were certainly weighted slightly in favour of the Combined Fleet. Villeneuve's fleet was significantly larger than Nelson's and possessed substantially greater

LEFT ABOVE Nelson's funeral procession by Daniel Turner. 'He fell gloriously just as a Briton ought to die – he has gone to rest where neither war nor slaughter reach.'
LEFT BELOW Nelson's victories: an allegorical print from the Nelson Museum at Monmouth.

THE TIMES
For 7th NOVEMBER. 1805

BATTLE OF
TRAFALGAR

CAPTURE OF
FRENCH AND SPANISH FLEETS

DEATH OF NELSON
List of Killed and Wounded

fire power. There was no element of surprise in the British battle plan. Everything that both the British columns did could, and should, have been anticipated. Certainly Nelson benefited from the rough weather, but only because his sailors surmounted its difficulties more easily than the French and Spanish.

Even when things went wrong, the character and courage of the British sailors saw their Admiral through. Dumanoir's eight ships at the head of the column took two hours to enter the battle – their failure was perhaps decisive. The eight ships in the rear of the British fleet took just as long – but the out-numbered vessels already engaging the enemy were able to hold out. Collingwood's first eight ships fought seventeen of the enemy, captured five of them, drove two others out of the line and so badly crippled four more that they fell easy victims

THE TIMES.

LONDON,

URSDAY, NOVEMBER 7, 1805.

e Publication to the Newsmen finished this
ing at half-past seven.

he official account of the late naval
on, which terminated in the most de-
e victory that has ever been achieved
British skill and gallantry, will be
d in our paper of this day. That the
mph, great and glorious as it is, has
dearly bought, and that such was
general opinion, was powerfully
ced in the deep and universal afflic-
with which the news of Lord Nel-
s death was received. The victory
ed none of those enthusiastic emo-
in the public mind, which the suc-
of our naval arms have in every
er instance produced. There was
a man who did not think that the life
he Hero of the Nile was too great a
for the capture and destruction of
ty sail of French and Spanish men-
ar. No ebullitions of popular trans-
no demonstrations of public joy,
ed this great and important event.
honest and manly feeling of the peo-
appeared as it should have done;
felt an inward satisfaction at the
ph of their favourite arms; they
ned with all the sincerity and poig-
y of domestic grief their Hero slain.

the official detail we are enabled to
the following particulars respecting
eath of as great an Admiral as ever
ed the Naval thunder of Britain.
Lord Nelson found that by his
al manœuvres he had placed the
y in such a situation that they could
avoid an engagement, he displayed
tmost animation, and with his usual
ence of victory he said to Captain
y, and the officers who surrounded
on the quarter-deck, "Now they
st escape us; I think we shall at
make sure of twenty of them. I
probably lose a leg, but that will be
asing a victory cheaply." About
ours before the close of the action
ordship received a wound in the
der from a musket ball, which was
from the tops of the Santissima
adada, with which ship he was closely
zed. The ball penetrated his breast,
e instantly fell; he was immediately
d below, and the surgeons pro-
ced the wound mortal. His Lordship
ed the intelligence with all the firm-
and pious resignation to the will of
e, Providence, of which he has given
frequent and signal examples during
rilliant course of peril and of glory.
nmediately sent an Officer to Admiral
ngwood, the second in command, with
nstructions for continuing the action
h he had so gallantly commenced, and
nelancholy bequest of his last farewell.

ring the short interval between his
ving the wound and his final disso-

lution he remained perfectly collected
displaying in his last moments the heroism
that had marked every action of his
glorious life. In that trying moment, cut
off from nature and from glory's cause,
all his anxiety, all his thoughts, were
directed to his country and her fame.

A few minutes before he expired he
sent for Captain Hardy; when the Captain came he inquired how many of the
enemy's ships had struck. The Captain
replied that, as nearly as he could ascertain, fifteen sail of the line had struck
their colours. His Lordship then, with
that fervent piety which so strongly
marked his character, returned thanks to
the Almighty; then turning to Captain
Hardy he said, "I know I am dying.
I could have wished to have survived to
breathe my last upon British ground, but
the will of God be done!" In a few
moments he expired.

If ever there was a man who deserved
to be "praised, wept, and honoured,"
by his country, it is Lord Nelson. His
three great naval achievements have
eclipsed the brilliancy of the most dazzling
victories in the annals of English daring.
If ever a hero merited the honours of a
public funeral and a public mourning, it
is the pious, the modest, and the gallant
Nelson, the darling of the British Navy,
whose death has plunged a whole nation
into the deepest grief, and to whose
talents and bravery even the enemy he
has conquered will bear testimony.

The action appears to have been gallantly contested by the French and Spaniards. Their object in risking an encounter with such a fleet, commanded by
such a man, must have been one of im-
perious necessity at this moment; no less,
we suspect, than a bold effort to acquire
a complete ascendency in the Mediterranean. Had they succeeded in liberating
that portion of the Spanish Navy which
is confined to the port of Carthagena by
the bare apprehension of an English
Squadron, their united force would have
amounted to upwards of forty sail of line.
There are also some ships off Toulon, and
the Rochfort squadron, with its usual
success, might have perhaps also added its
troops to the combined force. With such
a port as Toulon to take refuge in, a fleet
of this extent, under Commanders of common capacity, must have occupied a very
large portion indeed of our naval strength.

We shall anxiously expect the details of
this glorious and important victory. We
trust that the apprehensions entertained
by Admiral Collingwood with respect to
the captured ships may not be realised,
and that a few of them, of the French at
least, may yet be added to the list of the
British Navy.

Captain Sykes, of the Nautilus, and
Lieutenant Lapenotiere, of the Pickle
schooner, arrived at the Admiralty together about half-past one o'clock yesterday morning. The former did not, as
was generally understood, arrive from the
scene of action; he fell in by accident
with the Pickle schooner, and on learning
the intelligence proceeded immediately to
Lisbon with the information, from whence
he was sent with dispatches, by Mr.
Gambier, the British Consul, to England, and landed at Plymouth. Lieutenant
Lapenotiere made the Port of Falmouth,
and, by a singular coincidence, met Captain Sykes at the gates of the Admiralty.
This active Officer was yesterday promoted
to the rank of Commander.

Immediately on the arrival of the dispatches, Lord Barham rose from his bed
to peruse them, and continued at business
till five o'clock, when a messenger was
sent off to his Majesty at Windsor.

Admiral Collingwood's conduct has
obtained the fullest approbation, and last
night dispatches were sent off to Plymouth to be forwarded to him by the
Acasta, containing a commission which
appoints him to the command of the ships
in the Mediterranean with the same powers
as Lord Nelson had.

The several ships of the line at Portsmouth and Plymouth are ordered to put
to sea without loss of time, to reinforce
Admiral Collingwood.

Besides those officers mentioned in the
Gazette as having fallen in the action,
Mr. Scott, Lord Nelson's Secretary, was
killed by a chain shot, which cut him
asunder.

There was a partial illumination
throughout the metropolis last night. A
general one will take place this evening.

NELSON AND COLLINGWOOD.

"England expects every man will do his duty."
NELSON'S LAST TELEGRAPH.

I.

Britons! you heard Trafalgar's story,
You triumph in your country's glory,
Mourn o'er the relics pale and gory,
    Of brave, immortal Nelson.
To earth and war our Hero's dead,
To Heaven and peace his spirit fled;
Twine your green Laurels round the head
    Of brave, immortal Nelson.
        Mourn, one and all,
        Great Nelson's fall,
Oh! dash not off the gushing tear;
        No tears disgrace
        The manly face,
When freeman tends a freeman's bier.
Fame's rugged steep with daring feet he trod,
True to his King, his Country, and his God!

II.

When Passion's slave and Fortune's minion,
Panting to spread usurped dominion,
To Egypt flew, on vulture pinion,
    Lo! there immortal Nelson,
To check the conquest of the world,
Old Nilus hail'd our flag unfurled;
Wide havoc on the Gaul was hurl'd
    By brave, immortal Nelson.
        Lord of the main,
        He sail'd again;
    Where Copenhagen's rampart's tow'r'd
        Gaul's mad intrigues
        And captious leagues,
    Break in the tempest Nelson pour'd.
In Briton's cause he bore the avenging rod,
But gave the glory to Almighty God!

III.

Each change of atmosphere disdaining,
With scarce the wreck of health remaining,
Never of toil or wound complaining,
    Serv'd brave, immortal Nelson.
Trafalgar saw the warrior dight
Conspicuous of the hottest fight,
Foremost to guard Britannia's right,
    Sprang brave, immortal Nelson.
        With heart elate
        He met his fate,
    And calmly mark'd life's ebbing sand;
        Said, with a sigh,
        He wished to die,
    In dear Britannia's favour'd land.
But Death's dark path with Christian faith he trod,
And bow'd submissive to the Throne of God!

IV.

Mourn and rejoice! Horatio's spirit,
Well pleased, beholds a friend inherit
The honours paid to valour's merit,
        He smiles on gallant Collingwood.
Mourn for your martyrs on the wave,
Mourn for your Nelson in his grave,
Rejoice and cheer the living brave,
        With modest, gallant Collingwood.
        United raise
        Loud hymns of praise,
Your prayers, your thanks are due to Heav'n;
        Your loss deplore,
        That tribute o'er,
Be grateful for the champions given. [trod,
By their great Admiral's side Fame's path they
True to their King, their Country, and their God!

LORD NELSON'S LAST MOMENTS.

When Lord Nelson was shot, and was yet in
the arms of the men who were supporting him,
his eye caught the tiller rope, which was unusually
slack; he exclaimed, with much emphasis,
"Tighten that rope there!" an eminent proof that
his professional ardour still survived the brilliancy
of the flame of life. When he saw his Secretary
and his friend, Mr. Scott, thrown overboard,
uncertain of the disfigurement of the wound and
the confusion of the fight whether it was him or
not, he inquired, with affectionate ardour—"Was
that poor Scott?" An impression seems to be
made on Lord Nelson, for as the men were
carrying him down to the cockpit he said—
"Don't let me be thrown overboard; tell Hardy
to carry me home."

A man was so completely cut in two by a
double-headed shot, that the whole of his body,
with the exception of his legs up to his knees,
was blown some yards into the water; but,
strange to tell, his legs were left standing on the
deck with all the firmness and animation of life!

A midshipman, of the name of Price, was
brought into the cockpit, with his leg cut off up
to the calf; he was an heroic youth of 17. The
surgeons could not attend to him at the moment.
He drew out a knife, and cut off a piece of flesh
and the splinter of the bone with great compo-
sure. "I can stay," said he; "let me doctor
myself." When the surgeon attended him it was
found necessary to amputate above the knee. He
submitted to the operation without a groan.
"It is nothing at all," he said; "I thought it
had become much worse."

when reinforcement arrived. Trafalgar was a battle planned by officers but won by sailors.

The sailors had all felt 'the Nelson touch'. They had shared and gloried in his previous victories. At Trafalgar they were the architects of his greatest triumph and they were devastated by his death. Aboard the *Royal Sovereign*, a seaman wrote during the night after the battle had ended:

Our dear Admiral Nelson is killed! So we have paid pretty sharply for licking 'em. I never set eyes on him for which I am both sorry and glad – for to be sure I should like to have seen him – but then, all the men in our ship who have seen him are such soft toads, they have done nothing but blast their eyes and cry. Bless you! chaps that fought like the devil sit down and cry like a wench.

For the entire fleet the despair at the loss they had sustained transcended joy in the victory they had won. Hardy's letter home expressed the mood of the fleet exactly: 'We have on the 21st Instant obtained a most Glorious Victory over the Combined Fleets, but it has cost the Country a life that no money can replace, and one for whose Death I shall for ever mourn.' Codrington of the *Orion* declared that: 'There never was such a Combat since England had a Fleet' and that this had been 'the greatest victory in our annals'. Yet nothing could reconcile 'the irreparable loss of the greatest Admiral England ever knew'. Aboard the *Royal Sovereign*, a Midshipman wrote: 'He fell gloriously just as a Briton ought to die – he has done his duty to his Country and has gone to rest where neither war nor slaughter reach.'

Admiral Collingwood wrote to the British Minister in Naples in much the same tone:

The most decisive and complete Victory ever gained over a powerful Enemy. . . . The Combined Fleet is annihilated. I believe there are not more than four or five Ships in Cadiz which can be made ready for sea. . . . Yet this great event has been the cause of far more lamentation than joy. Never did any man's death cause so universal a sorrow as Lord Nelson's.

Coleridge recorded how universal that sorrow was:

When Nelson died it seemed as if no man was a stranger to another: for all were made acquaintances in the rights of a common anguish. Never can I forget the sorrow and consternation that lay on every countenance. . . . Numbers stopped and shook hands with me, because they had seen the tears on my cheek, and conjectured that I was an Englishman; and some, as they held my hand, burst themselves, into tears.

The return of Nelson's body to England, the funeral procession that stretched across London, the Court mourning and the public grief are remembered in Britain as a great expression of national gratitude. But they were more than that. They were an expression of national affection. Nelson had become more than the authentic hero of modern British history. He had become accepted by the nation as he was by the Navy as 'the man to love'.

The Trafalgar medal. 'We have on the 21st Instant obtained a most Glorious Victory over the Combined Fleets, but it has cost the Country a life that no money can replace.'

to my Country'

THE VICTORY OF TRAFALGAR was a turning point in European history. After the defeat of the Combined Fleet off Cadiz, the war against Napoleon was confined to continental Europe. Invasion of England was neither a prospect for France nor a threat to Britain. The Board of Admiralty in Whitehall decided who could sail up the Channel, through the Mediterranean or on the North Sea. The naval supremacy which Nelson established secured Britain's insular independence for over a hundred years. That single epoch-changing achievement would in itself have justified Nelson's reputation for all time. It would have explained all the inn-signs and the place-names, all the traditions that the Navy either inherited from Nelson or invented and later attributed to their most famous sailor.

But that crowning achievement was only one of the ingredients of Nelson's abiding reputation as Britain's authentic hero. Of course, his sudden death at the moment of victory produced a wave of anguish and a surge of adoration which made an immense contribution to the lasting idolatry. But if he had died in Matcham, full of years and surrounded by Emma's children, he would have occupied much the same place in history. It was his life not his death that set him apart. The life all of a piece: a plan which led inexorably to Trafalgar. It was a life committed to glory. That is how the world sees it in retrospect and it is how Nelson saw it at the time.

Nelson was triumphantly dedicated to the fulfilment of what he knew to be his destiny. The discovery of the vocation to which God had been pleased to call him came early in life. At the age of seventeen he first saw the 'radiant orb' which later led him from victory to victory. A year later, he felt the 'sudden glow of patriotism' and determined 'to be a hero and brave every danger'. For the next thirty years, he was as good as his word.

Perhaps the tales of boyhood bravery are apocryphal. Perhaps the pursuit of the Arctic bear was simply adolescent bravado. But from the moment young Captain Nelson chose to join the inland expedition against Fort San Juan in Nicaragua, he was always willing to risk cypresses in the hope of winning laurels. He saw life in exactly those terms when he lost his arm at Santa Cruz. The alternative appears again when he chased the French fleet from one end of the Mediterranean to the other in order that he could meet and beat them

PREVIOUS PAGES Nelson's funeral procession leaves Greenwich Hospital, 8 January 1806.

OPPOSITE The death of Nelson. 'Britannia mourns, George IV succours and immortality awaits.'

Immortality

VICTORY

VIVE L'EMP... FRANÇOIS

Bay of ...
Trafalgar...

Jᵒ Gillray Invᵗ & fᵗ   Publish'd Decʳ 23 1805 by H Humphrey 27 Sᵗ Jamesˢ

_ the Death of ADMIRAL·LORD·NELSON, in the moment of Victory! _

this Design for the Memorial intended by the City of London to commemorate the Glorious Death of the immortal
Nelson, is with every sentiment of respect, humbly submitted to the Right honᵇˡᵉ the Lord Mayor & the Court of Aldermen

'The Immortal Memory'

The adoration which surrounded Nelson after his death – and which has not ceased – was at once expressed in the production of a vast quantity of mementoes – monuments, portraits, inscribed china and snuff-boxes.

RIGHT The death of Nelson; a Staffordshire group.

BELOW A Nile snuff-box showing the *L'Orient* on fire and about to explode.

RIGHT Nelson looks towards
France from Trafalgar
Square. The statue, nearly
eighteen feet tall and carved
from Craigleath stone, was
erected in 1843. It was the
work of the sculptor
E.H. Bailey.

RIGHT The *Victory*: the quarter-deck looking aft over the place where Nelson fell.
BELOW The *Victory*: the lower gun deck.

in the bay outside Alexandria. At Bastia and Calvi he chose to fight on land like a marine. At Santa Cruz, despite the advice of his stepson, he chose to land with the shore party. Wherever there was a choice, some force within him always insisted that he must be where the action was hottest. Modern psychology may provide a dozen possible explanations for the irresistible compulsion. Some may prove that courage has strange causes, but the facts of the heroism are beyond dispute.

In part, the heroism produced the famous victories. At Cape St Vincent, 'Nelson's patent bridge for boarding first rates' was built on his willingness to leap from his own ship to the *San Nicholas* and then leap again from the *San Nicholas* to the *San Josef*. At Aboukir Bay, the French were confounded because Nelson risked taking his ships through uncharted shoals. On each occasion he made the hero's choice – or chose what, to most ordinary men, would have seemed the heroic alternative. For Nelson only one course was possible: 'If a man consults whether he is to fight when he has the power in his own hands it is certain that his opinion is against fighting.' Nelson never consulted. The decision to fight was an automatic response. Sometimes the desire overcame judgment. More often the instinct proved right. At any rate, it was instinct that guided him – instinct for what he believed to be success in the pursuit of honour. In 1781 he ungraciously brushed aside Admiral Digby's welcome to North America – 'a fine station for making prize money' – with a complaint that he wanted 'a station of honour'. Honour meant glorious victory. That was the only definition of the word that interested Nelson.

It is generally held that loyalty and obedience are essential ingredients of the honour that is won by bearing arms. Nelson was loyal and obedient according to his own judgment and convenience. It is impossible to argue that the repudiation of the truce negotiated with the Jacobins in Naples was anything but a deeply dishonourable act or that the execution of Caracciolo was anything but a travesty of honourable justice. Nelson's disloyalty to those superiors for whom he had little respect (in sharp distinction to the loyalty he expected to receive) demonstrated at best an unattractive egocentricity. The letters home complaining of the inadequacies of Admiral Hyde Parker are excusable and understandable. The signal to the Admiralty reporting that the elderly Commander-in-Chief

Victory Oct. 19: 1805
Noon Cadiz ESE 16 Leagues

My Dearest beloved Emma the dear
friend of my bosom the signal has
been made that the Enemys combined
fleet are coming out of Port, We
have very little Wind so that I have
no hopes of seeing them before to morrow
May the God of Battles crown my
endeavours with success at all events
I will take care that my name shall ever
be most dear to you and Horatia both
of whom I love as much as my own
life, and as my last writing before the
battle will be to you so I hope in God that
I shall live to finish my letter after the

was reluctant to sail north because of his recent marriage was not, and is certainly not, excused by the later sentimental assurances that, however the battle of Copenhagen was to be fought, Nelson would remain a loyal second-in-command.

In fact, in all these matters Nelson possessed the most extraordinary double standards. His criticisms of superiors he believed to be inadequate are in sharp contrast to his attitude when others criticised his performance, questioned his authority or slighted his seniority. In 1799, in the Levant, he thought it impossible to accept the orders of Sidney Smith who was 'lower in the list' and wrote to the Admiralty to say so. In the West Indies, ten years earlier, he had disrupted the colonial administration for weeks rather than allow a retired officer to fly the broad pennant which would imply that Nelson must accept his orders.

While he sentimentally reprieved Seaman Clark, there were other mutineers he would have gladly 'hanged on Christmas Day'. He always chose when to apply the principles and accept the rules which others believed to be universally appropriate. In his personal life, the rules were almost always broken, the principles ignored and the conventions flouted.

There are a dozen possible explanations as to why Nelson first neglected and then abandoned his wife. His relationship with Emma Hamilton – which moves from infatuation to obsession – is open to at least as many interpretations. One thing is, however, certain. The standards of the society in which he moved were flouted and broken in a way which was squalid as well as flagrant.

For nearly ten years, the behaviour of Lady Hamilton and Lord Nelson dominated the gossip of their friends. No one doubted the nature or the intensity of the relationship. Nelson's comrades-in-arms knew and generally disapproved. The Board of Admiralty kept him afloat and so away from Emma. Captain Troubridge begged that he should 'leave off'. Captain Hardy, promised land and a pension from the Bronte estate, hesitated to accept as he profoundly disapproved of Nelson's Neapolitan adventures. Eventually, however, even Nelson's own family accepted the existence of the strange triangular relationship that meant that William Hamilton was simultaneously Nelson's patron and cuckold. They could hardly have done anything else. It was permanent to the point of being institutionalised. Nelson could not have kept it secret. On shore, he had no other wish than to be with Emma

The first page of Nelson's last letter to Emma Hamilton, 'a legacy to my King and Country'.

Hamilton. Out of her sight, he was haunted by the fear of her infidelity. The strength of his obsession made discretion impossible. But although his behaviour was flagrant, he tried – foolishly and unsuccessfully – to keep it all a secret.

That was the squalid side of the affair. The pointless lies and the childish attempts at deception all failed. The complicated messages sent in the name of a befriended sailor and the altar-rail vows that, since the relationship was pure, Horatia could not be their child, deceived no one. All the dissembling was unsuccessful. But it was attempted nevertheless. It is fortunate for Nelson's memory that the lies were found out. Had the attempted deceits succeeded, many historians would have judged Nelson lacking in both constancy towards his wife and courage on behalf of his mistress. Because the attempts at secrecy were pathetically unsuccessful, Emma and Horatio ('in love and proud of it') have passed into history with a reputation they hardly deserve. Their relationship was strong as frenzy is often strong, but it was not heroic. As there was so much more heroism in Nelson's life, romantic biographers have passed swiftly through the Neapolitan Court and kept the hero's memory intact.

When Charles Stuart Parnell's adultery removed him from the leadership of the Irish Party in 1890, William Ewart Gladstone – the most upright of all British Prime Ministers – recalled that as a boy he had read Southey's *Life of Nelson*. How, he wondered, did the biography deal with 'the tender points', for the Grand Old Man recalled that the book had been published by the Society for Promoting of Christian Knowledge.

Fate and, in consequence, history were kind. But in a very real sense Nelson made his own fate and, therefore, determined the tone as well as the facts of the history that was written around them. The tendency to ignore orders with which he did not agree can hardly be held against an Admiral who won two major victories by flagrant disobedience. At Cape St Vincent, the Spanish line was breached successfully because Nelson pulled out of the tight formation which Jervis had planned and ordered; a clear breach of naval discipline Jervis agreed to a complaining officer – 'and if ever you commit such a breach of your orders I will forgive you also'. At Copenhagen, the disobedience was even more blatant. Not least because it was the public knowledge of Nelson's junior officers. Once again the Commander-in-Chief was sympathetic. The battle was won because Nelson refused to acknowledge the signal to disengage. Later, Hyde Parker said, in mitigation of the offence, that it was made only to provide an excuse for withdrawal if Nelson needed one and that everyone knew that the signal would be ignored if Nelson wanted to continue the battle. With such sympathetic superiors to support him, Nelson's memory is impervious to the charge of indiscipline.

Indeed, the dash and daring that come from disobedience have helped to add the aura of heroism to the victories. The victories were in themselves important enough. Each one came at a moment of desperate national need. The timing was perfect. Each was achieved when the nation longed for success. Each turned the course of the war and ensured a British triumph in the following phase, but the fact of victory alone would not have made Nelson the object of national adoration which he became. It was the nature of the victories which did that. Bravery was their hallmark. But the quality of the metal on which that sign was printed was crucially important. Nelson was a professional sailor. He knew that courage alone did not bring victory. The technical ability and personal morale of the sailors he led were an equally essential ingredient. So, from his earliest days with the fleet, he worked hard to improve the competence and the conditions of the sailors who served under him. Trafalgar was the apotheosis of that principle turned into practice. While Nelson outnavigated Villeneuve, the British Navy outsailed the French and Spanish seamen. Having beaten them in the race across the Atlantic and back, they returned to Europe more willing and more able to fight, and when the fight came, they shot straighter and fired faster. In part, that was because Nelson believed in practice and preparation. It was also because of the heart he had put into the fleet by the provision of improved food, continuous activity and the constant reminder that they were part of a great enterprise. The officers – who were for fifty years to boast that they had been in the 'Band of Brothers' who fought the battle of Trafalgar – became involved in victory because they were associated with the plans that brought it about. The sailors became committed to success because Nelson not only treated them as human beings, but told them that they were human beings on whom the fate of Britain, and perhaps the fate of Europe, depended.

By the time the battle of Trafalgar came, the whole Navy

'Nelson and his Tars'
by Thomas Rowlandson.

ADMIRAL NELSON *recreating*

Verse 1.ˢᵗ Dammy Jack what a Gig what a true British whim
Let the fiddles strike up on the Main
What Seaman would care for an Eye or a limb
To fight o'er the Battle again.

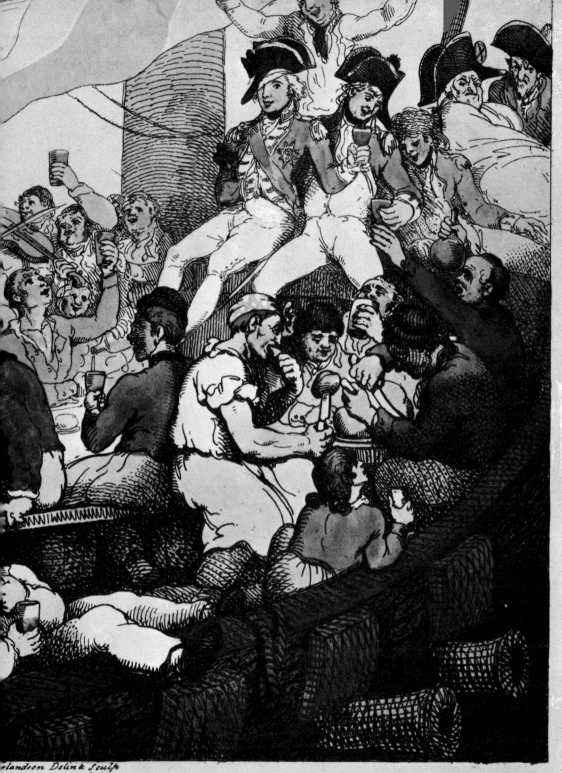

Rowlandson Delin & Sculp

Brave Tars after the GLORIOUS BATTLE of the NILE

Put the Bumpers about & be gay   *Verse 2.* See their tricolour'd rags how they're doft?
hear how our Doxies will smile   To shew that were Lords of the Sea.
Here's to *Nelson* for ever Huzza"   While the standard of England is flying aloft
ing George on the Banks of the Nile.   Come my Lads let us cheer it with Three.

felt the 'Nelson touch'. Its mysticism – Nelson's unshakeable belief in himself and in his sailors which he transmitted some-how to the fleet – certainly produced reserves of daring and determination that might not have been drawn out by a less self-confident leader. Because Nelson was inspired, he had the ability to inspire others. But that ability is not the whole story of the hold he had over the fleet. They knew that he took the business of fighting seamanship seriously. They saw him spend all night in a long-boat sounding the depths of the icy northern waters before he risked the dash through the shallows that won the battle of Copenhagen. They enjoyed the fresh fruit which he sought out on their behalf. They knew that a crew and its captain should feel committed to each other and that at the end of a voyage he wanted to keep them with him as much as they wanted to stay. The sailors on the *Foudroyant* who wrote to him 'with extra grief that we see you are about to leave us' knew that the grief would be shared by their Admiral. Nelson felt involved with his sailors, and his naval techniques worked on their behalf in every way. By 1805 they could recall that his combination of high professionalism and high courage usually ended with a minimum of battle casualties. That is how it worked out in Aboukir Bay in 1798. It was the same outside Cadiz seven years later. Once the Navy came to believe in Nelson, his victories and his reputation were assured. Nelson had no doubts about his own capabilities. He had implicit faith in the purpose of his life, in the inevitability of his death and in the obligation of posterity both to remember and to revere him. He worked hard to make those beliefs a reality and his success was a victory for application as well as for inspiration. But above all, it was a triumph for certainty. He believed devoutly that he was the authentic hero of British history. That is what he became.

Select Bibliography

E. Brenton, *The Naval History of Great Britain* (1823)

E. Brenton, *The Life and Correspondence of the Earl of St Vincent*, 2 Volumes (1838)

J. S. Corbett, *Campaign of Trafalgar* (1910)

Sir W. M. James, *Old Oak. The Life of John Jervis, Earl of St Vincent* (1950)

William James, *The Naval History of Great Britain, 1793-1820* (1837)

L. Kennedy, *Nelson's Band of Brothers* (1951)

M. A. Lewis, *The Social History of the Royal Navy, 1793-1815* (1960)

C. C. Lloyd, *Battles of St Vincent and Camperdown* (1963)

A. T. Mahon, *The Influence of Sea Power upon the French Revolution and Empire* 2 Volumes (1892)

A. T. Mahon, *The Life of Nelson* (1897)

Rene Maine, *Trafalgar – Napoleon's Naval Waterloo* (1957)

G. J. Marcus, *A Naval History of England, Volume 2 : The Age of Nelson* (1971)

Piers Mackesy, *The War in the Mediterranean, 1803-1810* (1957)

Carola Oman, *Nelson* (1947)

Tom Pocock, *Nelson and his World* (1968)

O. A. Sherrard, *A Life of Lord St Vincent* (1933)

R. Southey, *Life of Nelson* (1813)

Rear-Admiral A. H. Taylor, *Trafalgar* (Mariner's Mirror- Journal of the Society for Nautical Research, 1950)

Oliver Warner, *A Portrait of Lord Nelson* (1958)

Oliver Warner, *Trafalgar* (1959)

Oliver Warner, *The Battle of the Nile* (1960)

Oliver Warner, *Nelson and the Age of Fighting Sail* (1963)

Oliver Warner, *Nelson's Battles* (1965)

Oliver Warner, *The Life and Letters of Vice-Admiral Lord Collingwood* (1965)

Oliver Warner, *Great Sea Battles* (1963)

Clennell Wilkinson, *Nelson* (1931)

List of Illustrations

The author and publishers would like to thank the museums, agencies and photographers listed below for supplying the illustrations.

216

217

219

Picture research by Penny Brown

Index